The MAILBOX®

The Education Center®

Thematic Fun
for Little Learners

Preschool

Y0-AQH-072

Activities for preschoolers of all ages!

- Literacy
- Math
- Writing
- Science
- Social Studies
- Songs
- Art
- Fine Motor
- Gross Motor
- Snacks

Managing Editor: Kimberly Ann Brugger

Editorial Team: Becky S. Andrews, Margaret Ann Aumen, Diane Badden, Melissa Ballard, Amy Brinton, Kimberley Bruck, Ann Bruehler, Karen A. Brudnak, Marie E. Cecchini, Pam Crane, Chris Curry, Kathryn Davenport, Roxanne LaBell Dearman, Beth Deki, Brenda Fay, Pierce Foster, Deborah Garmon, Ada H. Goren, Karen Guess, Tazmen Hansen, Donna Harper, Erica Haver, Marsha Heim, Lori Z. Henry, Debra Liverman, Kitty Lowrance, Laura Mihalenko, Mary Ellen Moore, Tina Petersen, Mark Rainey, Greg D. Rieves, Mary Robles, Hope Rodgers, Rebecca Saunders, Donna K. Teal, Rachael Traylor, Sharon M. Tresino, Lynn Wagoner, Carole J. Watkins, Zane Williard

www.themailbox.com

Table of Contents

What's Inside

210 activities for 35 popular themes!

Need activities for early preschoolers? Just look for the ▢.

71 pages of timesaving reproducibles

All About Me

Social studies: Place a full-length mirror lengthwise against a wall and then angle the mirror so that youngsters can see themselves when they sit in front of it. Invite three or four little ones to sit in front of the mirror. Then name an emotion, such as happy or frightened, and prompt students to make faces in the mirror to show that emotion.

Literacy: Place letter tiles, magnetic letters, and foam letters in your sand table and provide access to student name cards. A child finds her name card. She searches through the sand to find the letters in her name and places them below the card. If desired, she repeats the process with classmates' name cards.

Math: Cut out a copy of an eye card from page 6 for each child. Have him look in a mirror and determine his eye color. Then encourage him to color his eye card to match. Attach the hook side of a small piece of self-adhesive Velcro fastener to the back of each card. Then place the eyes on a flannelboard. Prompt students to sort the eyes into groups by color.

Thematic Fun for Little Learners • ©The Mailbox® Books • TEC61310

Writing: Give each child a copy of page 7. Help him mount a photo of himself on the page. Then help him fill in the blanks to give his name, hair color, eye color, and height. This is sure to be a cherished keepsake for parents!

Josh
My hair is _brown_.
I have _green_ eyes.
I'm _3'7"_,
Just the right size!

Thematic Fun for Little Learners • ©The Mailbox® Books • TEC61310

Song: Lead students in performing this adorable action song that reinforces body part names.

(sung to the tune of "If You're Happy and You Know It")

I have eyes that help me see all around.   Touch eyes.
I have ears that let me hear every sound.   Touch ears.
I have fingers, I have toes,   Wiggle fingers; point to toes.
And one very special nose.   Touch nose.
And my feet help me to walk across the ground.   Walk in place.

Fine motor: Draw four heads and shoulders on a sheet of bulletin board paper and label them as shown. Attach the paper to a tabletop. Place scraps of red, yellow, brown, and black paper in a tub and provide several pairs of scissors. Youngsters tear or cut the scraps as desired and then glue them to the appropriate head to make hair. Encourage each youngster to point to the head that has a hair color similar to her own!

Eye Cards

Use with the third idea on page 4.

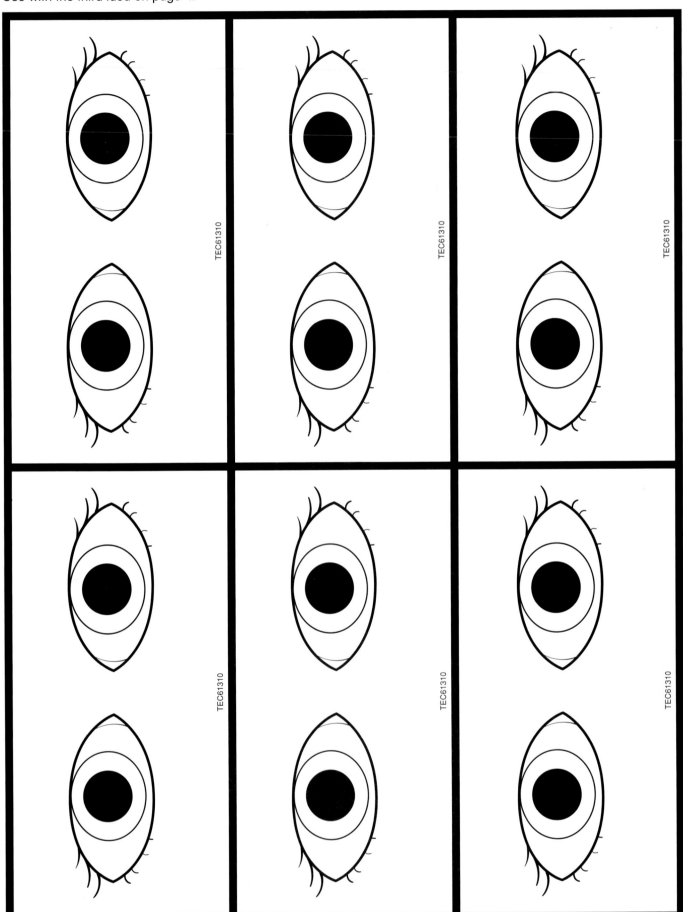

 Thematic Fun for Little Learners • ©The Mailbox® Books • TEC61310

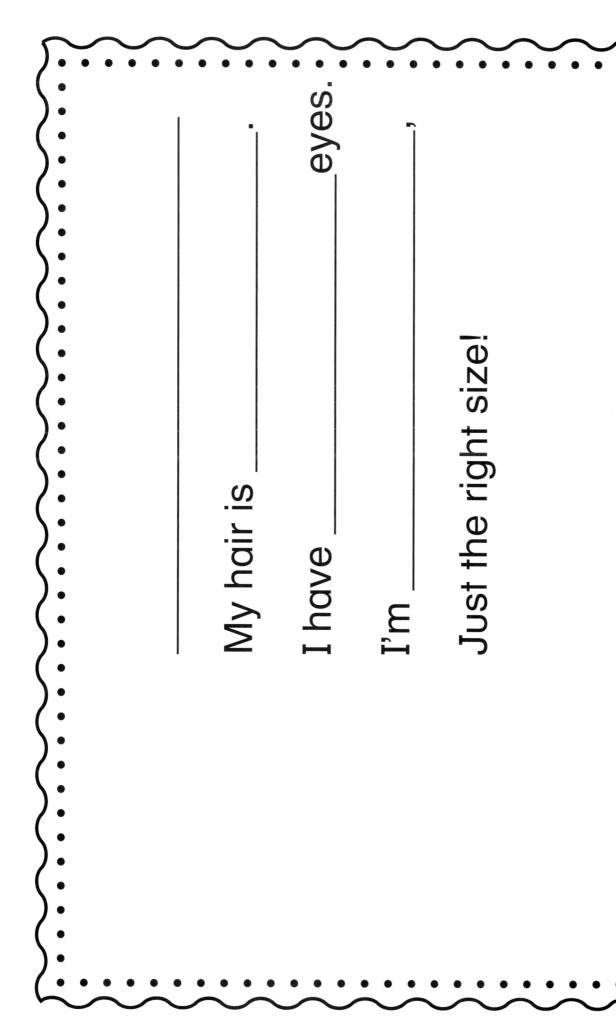

My hair is _____.

I have _____ eyes.

I'm _____,

Just the right size!

Thematic Fun for Little Learners • ©The Mailbox® Books • TEC61310

Note to the teacher: Use with the first idea on page 5.

Apples

Writing: Explain that Johnny Appleseed was a man who lived long ago and loved to grow apple trees. Next, give each youngster a copy of page 10. Have her write her name in the space provided. Then encourage her to color the page and draw a picture of her favorite type of food that has apples as an ingredient. Write the name of her food to complete the sentence. Then bind the pages together with a cover labeled "Thank You, Johnny Appleseed!"

_____ Sarah _____ loves _____ applesauce _____. Yes, indeed!
Thank you, Johnny Appleseed!

Song: Give each child a red disposable plate (apple) to use as a hand drum. Prompt youngsters to tap their apples as they sing this catchy song!

(sung to the tune of "Twinkle, Twinkle, Little Star")

Apple, apple on the tree,
I know you are good for me.
You are fun to munch and crunch
For a snack or in my lunch.
Apple, apple on the tree,
I know you are good for me!

Snack: To make this simple apple parfait, place a spoonful of apple pie filling (or finely chopped apples) in a plastic cup. Put a dollop of vanilla yogurt over the filling. Then sprinkle granola over the yogurt. What a tasty treat!

Math: Enlarge and color a copy of page 11. Then place yellow, green, and red pom-poms (apples) on separate trees. Make simple instruction cards similar to the one shown to tell how many apples to "pick." A youngster chooses a card and names the number of red apples. He "picks" the appropriate number of red apples from the tree. Then he repeats the process with the yellow and green apples. He continues with several cards until there are no apples on the trees.

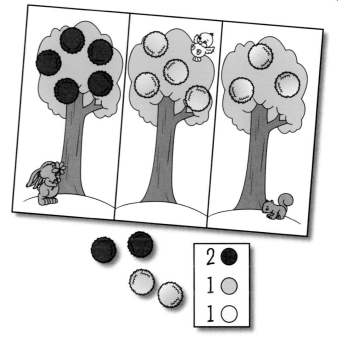

Science: Have each child color a copy of page 11. Explain that apple trees have blossoms in the spring. Prompt the child to glue crumpled pink tissue paper squares (blossoms) to the first tree. Then explain that the petals soon fall off the blossoms and what is left becomes little green apples. Encourage the child to glue green hole-punch dots (apples) to the second tree. Next, explain that the little green apples get larger and larger and then they turn red. Prompt the child to make red fingerprint apples on the final tree.

◻ Arts and crafts: Encourage each child to fingerpaint a large apple shape red. When he is satisfied with his work, he washes his hands. Then he cuts pieces of green yarn and presses them into the paint so they resemble worms. To finish his artwork, he glues a stem and leaf cutout to his apple.

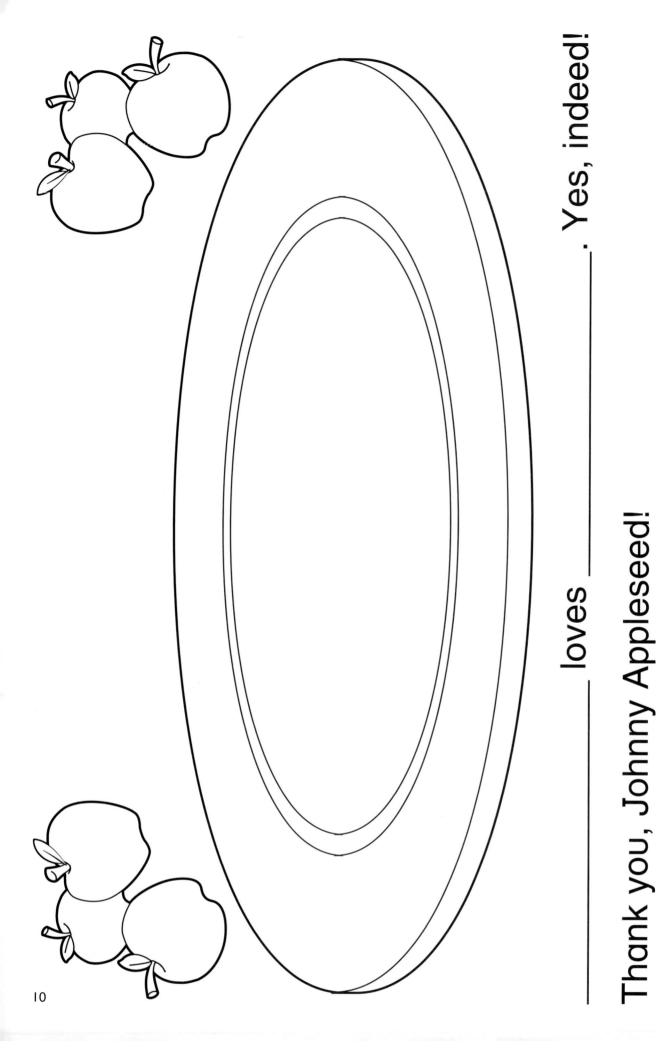

_____ loves _____ . Yes, indeed!

Thank you, Johnny Appleseed!

10

Note to the teacher: Use with the first activity on page 8.

═ **Note to the teacher:** Use with the first and second activities on page 9.

Pumpkins

Art: Place a pumpkin top, with stem attached, near a shallow pan of paint. Encourage a youngster to hold the top by the stem and dip it into the paint. Then prompt him to press the top on a sheet of paper. Have him continue in the same way until his paper is filled with pumpkin top prints. If desired, encourage him to sprinkle orange glitter over the wet paint.

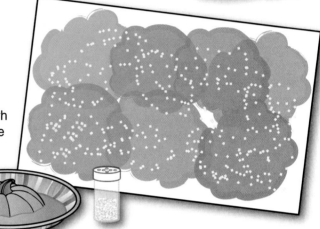

Literacy: Cut out a copy of the cards on page 14. Place the cards in a bag and place the bag near a hollowed-out pumpkin (or pumpkin cutout). Lead students in singing the song shown. Then have a child choose a card from the bag and identify the picture. Help the child determine whether the picture name begins with /p/ like *pumpkin*. If it does, have her drop the card in the pumpkin (or place the card on the pumpkin cutout). If not, have her set the card aside. Continue with each remaining card.

(sung to the tune of "Mary Had a Little Lamb")

Pumpkin starts with /p/, /p/, /p/,
/p/, /p/, /p/, /p/, /p/, /p/.
Pumpkin starts with /p/, /p/, /p/,
What else begins with /p/?

Math: Put large and small orange pom-poms (pumpkins) in a tub of green paper shreds or green tinted rice. Provide two containers, labeled as shown, and a pair of tongs (pumpkin pickers). A child uses the pumpkin pickers to pick a pumpkin and sorts it into the appropriate container. She continues until all the pumpkins have been picked and sorted.

Science: Cut out several copies of the cards on page 15. Gather a small pumpkin and a container of water. Ask youngsters whether they think a pumpkin will sink or float. Encourage each child to choose a card that shows his prediction. Gather the cards and encourage students to help you sort them and compare the results. Finally, place the pumpkin in the water. Then prompt students to revisit their predictions.

Song: Gather youngsters around a pumpkin and give each youngster a length of green crepe paper streamer (vine). Prompt youngsters to move the crepe paper through the air as you lead them in singing the song shown.

(sung to the tune of "Twinkle, Twinkle, Little Star")

Pumpkins, pumpkins on the vine,
Big and orange and oh so fine.
Some are fat; lopsided too;
Lumpy, bumpy, filled with goo!
Pumpkins, pumpkins on the vine,
Big and orange and oh so fine.

Alike	Different
round	squash is green
gooey on the inside	different sizes
has seeds	pumpkin has bigger seeds
can eat both	pumpkin is heavier

Literacy: Gather a pumpkin and a squash. (If desired, cut a hole in each one so that youngsters can observe and touch the interior.) Label a sheet of chart paper as shown. Then have students identify ways that the pumpkin and squash are alike and different. Write their thoughts on the chart paper.

Picture Cards

Use with the second idea on page 12.

TEC61310

TEC61310

TEC61310

TEC61310

TEC61310

TEC61310

TEC61310

TEC61310

TEC61310

TEC61310

TEC61310

TEC61310

Thematic Fun for Little Learners • ©The Mailbox® Books • TEC61310

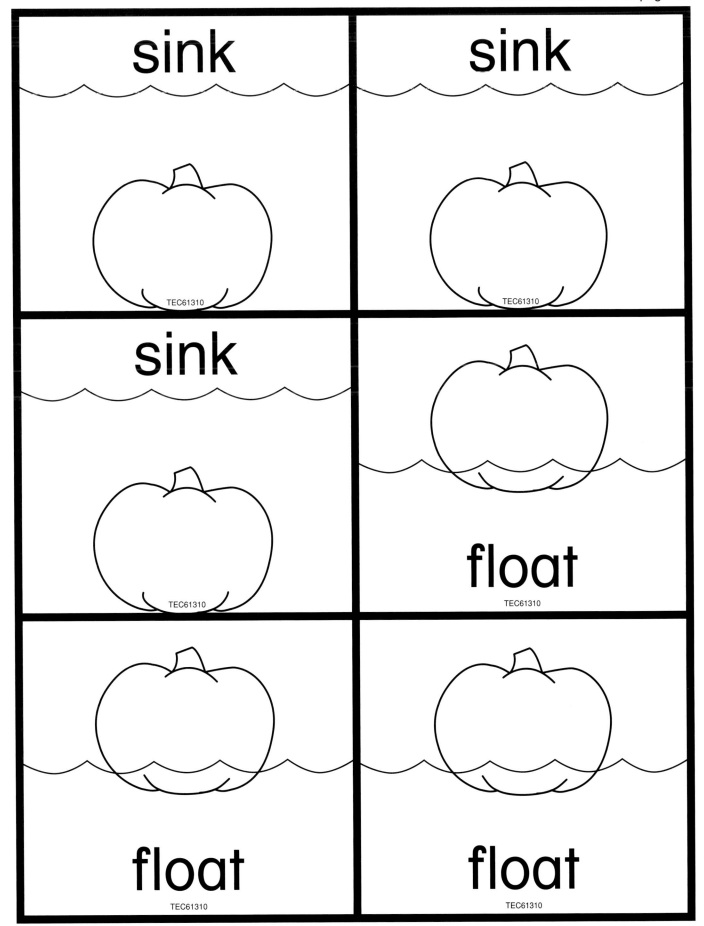

sink

sink

sink

float

float

float

Leaves

Literacy: Cut out several copies of the leaf patterns on page 18 and attach them to a tabletop in the shape of an *L*. Have a youngster visit the table, run his hand over the letter, and say, "/l/, /l/, leaf." Then help him attach a sheet of paper over the letter and rub an unwrapped crayon over the paper. Have him repeat the process with other crayons to create a lovely piece of artwork.

Math: Make a large tree shape out of poster board and gather number cards and a variety of fall leaves. A child chooses a number card and identifies the number. Then he places the appropriate number of leaves on the tree. He repeats the process with each remaining number card. What a lovely fall tree!

Art: Fill a few knee-high stockings with rice and then secure the opening of each one with a knot. Place each stocking near a shallow pan of paint. Give each child a sheet of paper with a tree trunk drawn on it. Then prompt her to hold the stocking by the knotted end and dip the rice-filled end into the paint. Have her lightly bounce the stocking on the paper to create fall foliage. Then encourage her to repeat the process with other colors of paint.

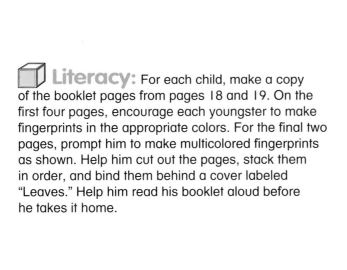

Literacy: For each child, make a copy of the booklet pages from pages 18 and 19. On the first four pages, encourage each youngster to make fingerprints in the appropriate colors. For the final two pages, prompt him to make multicolored fingerprints as shown. Help him cut out the pages, stack them in order, and bind them behind a cover labeled "Leaves." Help him read his booklet aloud before he takes it home.

Song: Give each youngster a length of crepe paper in a fall-related color. Then lead students in singing the song shown as they move their streamers through the air to make a whispering sound!

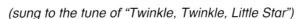

(sung to the tune of "Twinkle, Twinkle, Little Star")

"Whisper, whisper," say the leaves,
As they fall down from the trees.
They are orange and red and gold,
Looking frosty in the cold.
"Whisper, whisper," say the leaves,
As they fall down from the trees.

Math: Read aloud *Fall Leaves Fall!* by Zoe Hall. Then give each child a lunch bag and take the students outside to collect leaves. After youngsters return to the room, revisit the pages of the story that explain how leaves can be big or small, pointy or smooth. Next, have little ones place their leaves in a big pile. Put two plastic hoops on the floor and label the hoops as shown. Then help students sort the leaves by size. Next, change the headings to "pointy" and "smooth" and prompt students to re-sort the leaves.

Leaf Patterns

Use with the first activity on page 16.

Booklet Pages 1 and 2

Use with the first activity on page 17.

Orange,

1

yellow,

2

red,

3

and brown.

4

On my head

5

and on the ground.

6

Harvest

Gross motor: Color and cut out a copy of the cards on page 22. Tell little ones that many foods are harvested in the fall. Hold up a card and help students identify the food in the picture. Ask youngsters whether they have ever eaten the pictured food and whether they enjoy it. Then explain that people aren't the only ones that eat this food. Help students name the creature in the picture that is enjoying the food. Then have students move about the room as if they were that creature searching for and eating that particular food. Continue in the same way with each remaining card.

Literacy: Gather a few plastic (or real) vegetables, such as a potato, a yam, and a carrot. Seat students in a circle and give a child the potato. Prompt students to pass the potato around the circle as they chant, "Potato, potato, potato." Give a signal, such as ringing a chime or bell, for youngsters to stop. Help the child with the potato name another word that begins with /p/. Then prompt students to begin passing the potato again. Play several rounds of this game with each vegetable.

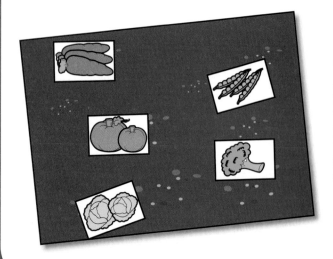

Literacy: Color and cut out a copy of the vegetable cards on page 23 and place them in a bag. Add soil details to a sheet of brown paper (garden) and place it on the floor. Have a child choose a card from the bag. Help her identify the vegetable on her card and place the card on the garden. Then lead youngsters in reciting the rhyme shown, prompting them to rub their tummies when they say, "Yum, yum, yum!" Continue with each remaining card.

> Veggies in the garden for us to eat.
> Yum, yum, yum—what a healthy treat!

Math: Here's an idea that results in a colorful Indian corn craft. Gather a small group of youngsters and give each child a construction paper corncob cutout. Provide bingo daubers in a variety of fall-related colors. Have students, in turn, roll a die and count the dots. Then encourage each child to choose a dauber and make a matching number of marks (kernels) on her corncob. Have youngsters continue until their corncobs are covered with colorful kernels.

Song: Lead students in performing this engaging action song about scarecrows!

(sung to the tune of "Old MacDonald Had a Farm")

Scarecrows scare away the crows.	*Stand like a scarecrow.*
Shoo, crows—fly away!	*Make shooing motions.*
They scare them from the corn that grows.	*Stand like a scarecrow.*
Shoo, crows—fly away!	*Make shooing motions.*
With a caw, caw here and a caw, caw there.	*Flap arms.*
Here a caw, there a caw, everywhere a caw, caw.	*Flap arms.*
Scarecrows scare away the crows.	*Stand like a scarecrow.*
Shoo, crows—fly away!	*Make shooing motions.*

Arts and crafts: To make this simple process art, use a foam paint roller to roll brown paint on a sheet of orange construction paper. Then use the tip of a carrot to draw lines in the paint. The carrot removes the brown paint and reveals the orange paper, giving the impression that you are drawing with the carrot!

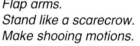

Picture Cards

Use with the first idea on page 20.

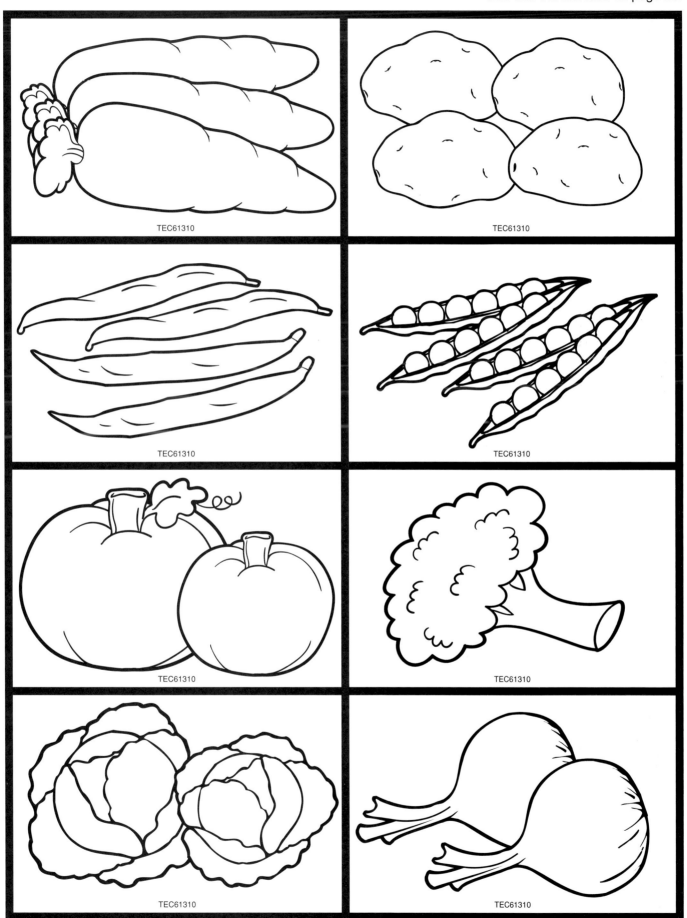

TEC61310

TEC61310

TEC61310

TEC61310

TEC61310

TEC61310

TEC61310

TEC61310

My Family

Literacy: Write several letters on your board, including a class supply of *F*s. Have a child locate an *F*, circle it, and say, *"F is for family!"* Prompt him to say something about his family, such as naming a game they like to play, a favorite movie they watch together, a place they like to go, or a family pet they own. Continue until each *F* has been circled.

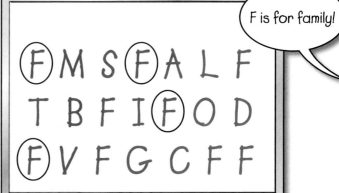

F is for family!

Social studies: Lead little ones in singing the song shown, prompting youngsters who have a brother to stand when indicated and then follow the actions given. Encourage students to help you count the number of children standing. Have the youngsters sit down. Then repeat the song several times, replacing the word *brother* with other family member names, such as *mother, father, sister, grandma,* and *grandpa.*

(sung to the tune of "Short'nin' Bread")

Do you have a [brother] in your family, family?
If you have a [brother], please stand up now!
Everybody standing, please wiggle, wiggle.   *Wiggle in place.*
Clap your little hands and then take a bow!   *Clap and then bow.*

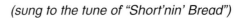

Arts and crafts: To make this family-friendly artwork, have each youngster fingerpaint a sheet of paper. Allow the paint to dry and then send the painting home with a copy of the note on page 26. When the finished artwork is sent back to school, have each child share his artwork with the class, explaining which family members helped create the masterpiece. Display these lovely projects in your classroom.

Math: Have each child bring a family photo to school. For protection, place each photo in a resealable plastic bag. Provide a variety of manipulatives, such as pom-poms, bear counters, stuffed animals, and blocks. Invite a child to the center and have her count the number of people in her family. Then encourage her to use the manipulatives to make other sets with the same number.

Song: Inspire little ones to talk about their families after they sing this cute song!

(sung to the tune of "Did You Ever See a Lassie?")

Will you talk about your family, your family, your family?
Will you talk about your family? We all want to hear!
Let's talk about mothers and sisters and brothers.
Will you tell us all about the ones that you hold dear?

Literacy: Give each child a copy of page 27. Have each youngster make handprints on the page as shown. Encourage her to name how she helps her family. Then write the information on the page. If desired, display the projects with youngsters' family photos.

Dear Family,

   Your youngster created this wonderful fingerpainting. Please join your child in adding family-made drawings and collage items to the artwork. Let your creativity shine! Please return the finished family masterpiece to school by _____.

Thank you very much!

_____

Dear Family,

   Your youngster created this wonderful fingerpainting. Please join your child in adding family-made drawings and collage items to the artwork. Let your creativity shine! Please return the finished family masterpiece to school by _____.

Thank you very much!

_____

Helping Hands

Turkeys

Math: Have students set a trap for turkeys by using a favorite turkey snack! Cut out a few copies of the turkey pattern on page 30 and set the cutouts aside. Scatter red and blue pom-poms (berries) around the room. Place two baskets on your floor. Then prompt youngsters to gather berries and sort them into the baskets by color. When youngsters have left for the day, conceal the baskets and scatter the turkey cutouts in their place. When youngsters arrive the next day, prompt students to notice that the turkeys have eaten all the berries!

Gross motor: Place a sheet of brown paper (nest) on the floor and invite a child (turkey) to sit on it. Then have the remaining youngsters stand in a circle around the turkey. Prompt little ones to tiptoe around the turkey as you lead them in singing the song shown. At the end of the song, have the turkey switch places with a classmate. Then repeat the song, replacing the word *tiptoe* with other gross-motor movements, such as *hop, march,* or *crawl.*

(sung to the tune of "Ring Around the Rosie")

[Tiptoe] around the turkey.
[Tiptoe] around the turkey.
[Tiptoe, tiptoe]—
We all stand still!

Arts and crafts: To make these colorful turkey tracks, cut a potato in half; then carve a turkey track in each half as shown. Place paper towels in two shallow containers; then saturate the paper towels in each container with a different color of paint. A child dips a potato half in paint and presses it on a sheet of paper. He repeats the process, adding more paint to the potato as needed and overlapping the prints as desired.

Turn to page 31 for a reproducible activity!

Math: Glue a turkey body cutout to the back of a paper plate. Then attach to the plate eight craft feathers arranged in an *AB* pattern. Place the turkey at a center along with a few more paper plate turkeys (minus the feathers). For each featherless turkey, provide the appropriate number and color of feathers to copy the pattern. A child takes a turkey and re-creates the pattern by placing the feathers in the correct color sequence around the edge of the plate.

Song: Youngsters will have a terrific time singing this toe-tapping turkey tune! After singing the song, ask little ones why they think Tom the turkey is hiding.

(sung to the tune of "Short'nin' Bread")

Chorus:
Where is Tom the turkey? He's hiding, hiding!
Where is Tom the turkey? He can't be found!
Where is Tom the turkey? He's hiding, hiding!
Where is Tom the turkey? He can't be found!

Look in the attic! Look in the shed!
Look in the cupboard and under the bed!
Look in the dresser! Look in the car!
Where is the turkey? He can't be far!

(Repeat chorus.)

Tobble, tobble, tobble!

Literacy: Have students say the word *turkey* and practice its beginning sound. Then ask each child to pretend he is a silly turkey. Tell your little gobblers to listen carefully as you announce a word. If the word begins with /t/ like *turkey*, youngsters strut around and say, "Tobble, tobble, tobble!" If the word begins with a different sound, students stand still. Continue in the same way.

Turkey Pattern

Use with the first activity on page 28.

Turkeys Are Terrific!

Cut.
Glue.

Thematic Fun for Little Learners • ©The Mailbox® Books • TEC61310

Note to the teacher: Help a student cut out the cards. Have her say each picture name and its beginning sound. Then have her glue to the page each picture whose name begins like *turkey*.

Penguins

Arts and crafts: Show youngsters a picture of a penguin and lead them to notice that the penguin is black and white. Next, encourage each child to attach a large penguin cutout (enlarged copy of the pattern on page 35) to a sheet of paper. Provide a variety of black-and-white collage items and prompt the child to glue the items around the penguin as desired.

Gross motor: Stand like a penguin with your arms (wings) at your sides and your feet together. Ask little ones to do the same, and then engage them in some fun penguin play. Recite the rhyme shown. At the end of the rhyme, lead your little penguins in waddling around the room. Then repeat the activity, replacing the word *waddle* with other gross-motor movements, such as *slide, swim, skate,* and *twirl.*

> Penguins, penguins,
> Watch what I do.
> I can [waddle].
> How about you?

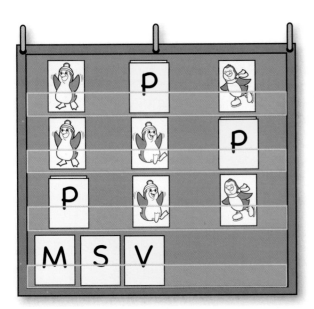

Literacy: Cut out a copy of the penguin cards on page 34 and place them in your pocket chart. Place letter cards in a bag, including 9 *P*s. Have a child choose a card and help him identify the letter. If it is a *P*, have him place the card over a penguin card and say, "/p/, /p/, penguin!" If it isn't a *P*, help him identify the letter and then place it at the bottom of the chart. Continue until each penguin is covered.

 # January

Literacy: To practice tracking print from left to right, have each child make a penguin stick puppet similar to the one shown (patterns on page 35). Then prompt youngsters to "skate" their penguins over writing found in your room, moving the penguin from left to right. For a different literacy option, have students "skate" their penguins around the room, pointing their puppets to any *P*s they may find.

Song: Your little penguins will love to waddle, slip, slide, swim, and dive as they sing this adorable song!

(sung to the tune of "Mary Had a Little Lamb")

Penguins waddle to and fro
On the ice,
On the snow.
They are always on the go.
They have a jolly time!

Penguins like to slip and slide
Down the hill,
On a ride.
Penguins like to swim and dive.
They have a jolly time!

Math: Give each child a copy of the large penguin cutout on page 35 and a cup of fish-shaped crackers. Have each child color the penguin. Then ask each student to guess how many crackers will fit on her penguin's tummy. Write down youngsters' guesses; then instruct each child to fill her penguin's tummy with crackers. Help each student count the crackers to determine how many actually fit and then compare the number of crackers to her estimate. Finally, invite your little penguins to nibble their fish!

Penguin Cards

Use with the third activity on page 32.

TEC61310

TEC61310

TEC61310

TEC61310

TEC61310

TEC61310

TEC61310

TEC61310

TEC61310

Penguin Pattern

Use with the first activity on page 32 and the third activity on page 33.

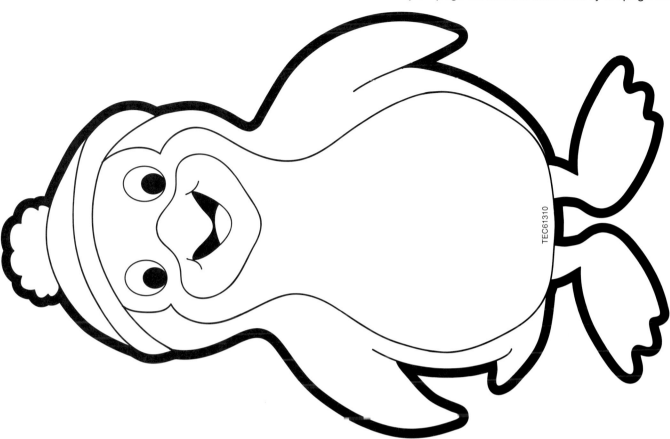

TEC61310

Skating Penguin Pattern

Use with the first activity on page 33.

TEC61310   TEC61310

Snow

Science: Give each child a white pom-pom (snowflake). Invite little ones to play a game of Snowman Sees. Pretend to be Snowman and say, "Snowman sees a snowflake falling on your elbow," prompting each child to gently "float" her snowflake to her elbow. Continue the activity with other body parts, challenging youngsters with less familiar words like *heel* and *shin*.

Snack: To make this snack, have each child spread white chocolate or vanilla pudding on a small plate so it resembles a snowdrift. Give each child animal-shaped cookies and encourage her to make one of the animals frolic in the snow. Then encourage her to eat the snow-covered cookie! Have her continue for each remaining cookie.

Math: Attach craft foam shapes (buttons) to several snowman cutouts (pattern on page 38). Provide a duplicate set of buttons for each snowman. Invite a child to choose a snowman. Encourage him to find matching buttons and then place them over the original buttons. He continues for each remaining snowman.

Math: Write random numbers on a sheet of paper and make a class supply of blue construction paper copies. Give each youngster in a small group a paper. Provide squares of white tissue paper and a shallow container of glue. Name a number. After each child finds the number on her paper, encourage her to crumple a tissue paper square, dip it in glue, and then press it on the number. When each number is covered, the paper resembles a snowstorm!

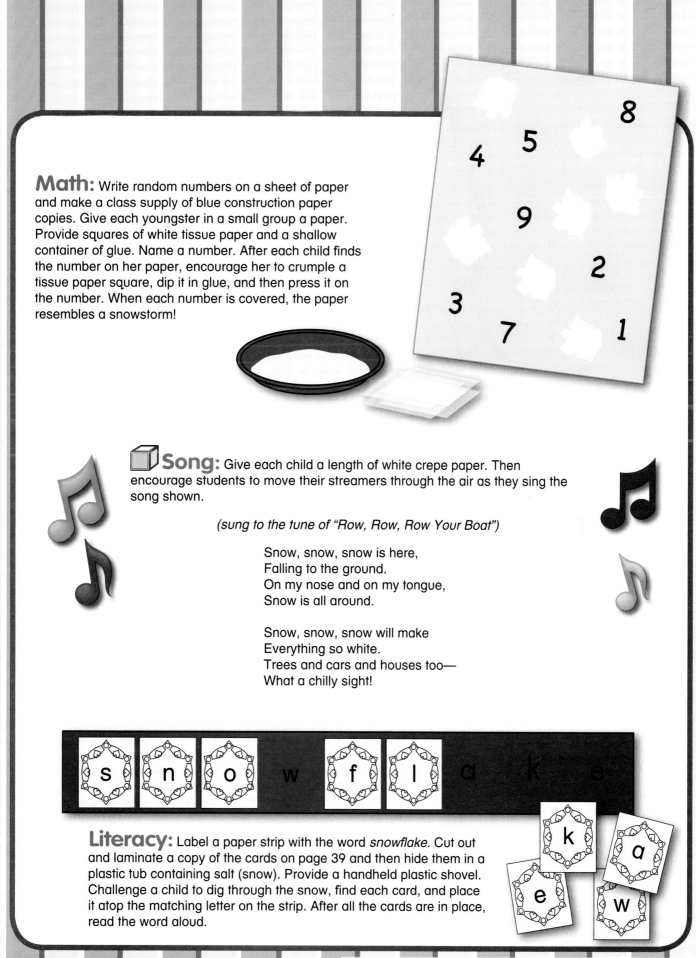

Song: Give each child a length of white crepe paper. Then encourage students to move their streamers through the air as they sing the song shown.

(sung to the tune of "Row, Row, Row Your Boat")

> Snow, snow, snow is here,
> Falling to the ground.
> On my nose and on my tongue,
> Snow is all around.
>
> Snow, snow, snow will make
> Everything so white.
> Trees and cars and houses too—
> What a chilly sight!

Literacy: Label a paper strip with the word *snowflake.* Cut out and laminate a copy of the cards on page 39 and then hide them in a plastic tub containing salt (snow). Provide a handheld plastic shovel. Challenge a child to dig through the snow, find each card, and place it atop the matching letter on the strip. After all the cards are in place, read the word aloud.

Snowman Pattern

Use with the third activity on page 36.

TEC61310

s

n

o

TEC61310

TEC61310

TEC61310

w

f

l

TEC61310

TEC61310

TEC61310

a

k

e

TEC61310

TEC61310

TEC61310

Literacy: Display a mitten and have students say its name, emphasizing the beginning sound. Then give youngsters a clue to help them guess another /m/ word. For example, you might say, "I am thinking of something white that you pour on cereal." After the word *milk* is guessed, have the group repeat the word, emphasizing its beginning sound. Continue the activity with other words that begin with /m/, such as *monkey, moon, mouse, mop,* and *money.*

Milk.

Math: Gather several different pairs of mittens (or cut out and decorate copies of the mitten patterns on page 42) and give one mitten from a pair to each child. Place the remaining mittens in a pile. Take a mitten from the pile and hold it in the air while you sing the song shown. At the end of the song, the child with the matching mitten holds her mitten next to yours. Set the pair aside. Then continue with the remaining mittens.

(sung to the tune of "The Muffin Man")

Oh, do you have the mitten match,
The mitten match, the mitten match?
Oh, do you have the mitten match
To make a mitten pair?

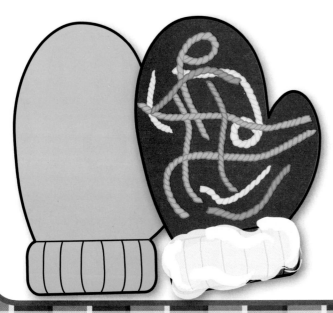

Arts and crafts: Set out construction paper mittens (patterns on page 42), yarn clippings, cotton batting, and glue. A youngster spreads glue on a mitten and then presses yarn clippings into the glue. Then he glues cotton batting to the cuff.

See page 43 for a reproducible activity!

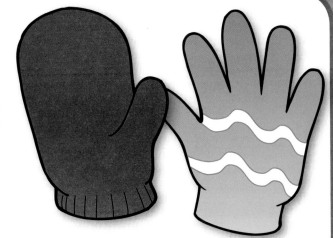

Literacy: For this oral language activity, have each child in a small group put on one mitten and one glove. Invite youngsters to discuss the similarities and differences between the two items. Next, ask each child to count the fingers on her gloved hand and then the fingers on her mittened hand. Encourage students to share what they discover. Finally, ask little ones to try holding hands in different ways—such as glove-to-glove, mitten-to-glove, and mitten-to-mitten—and discuss what happens.

 Song: Little ones will enjoy performing this simple action song!

(sung to the tune of "A Tisket, a Tasket")

My mitten, my mitten,	*Hold up hand and show a sad face.*
I lost my purple mitten!	
I had it right here yesterday,	*Shake finger.*
But now I think I lost it!	*Throw arms out to sides and shrug.*
My mitten, my mitten,	*Hold up hand and show a happy face.*
I found my purple mitten!	*Point to hand.*
I looked around, looked up and down,	*Shake finger.*
And found it in my pocket!	*Point to pocket.*
My pocket, my pocket,	*Point to pocket.*
I found it in my pocket!	
That purple mitten isn't lost.	*Shake finger.*
It's right here in my pocket!	*Point to pocket.*

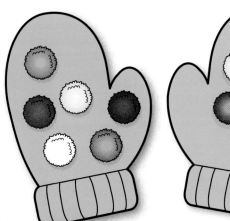

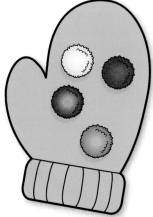

Math: For this partner activity, provide two mitten cutouts (patterns on page 42), a large die, and 12 pom-poms. Each youngster takes a mitten. In turn, each child rolls the die, counts the number of dots, and places that many pom-poms on his mitten. Then the partners compare the sets of pom-poms using the words *more, fewer,* or *equal.* For an added challenge, provide two dice and 24 pom-poms.

Mitten Patterns

Use with the second and third activities on page 40 and the third activity on page 41.

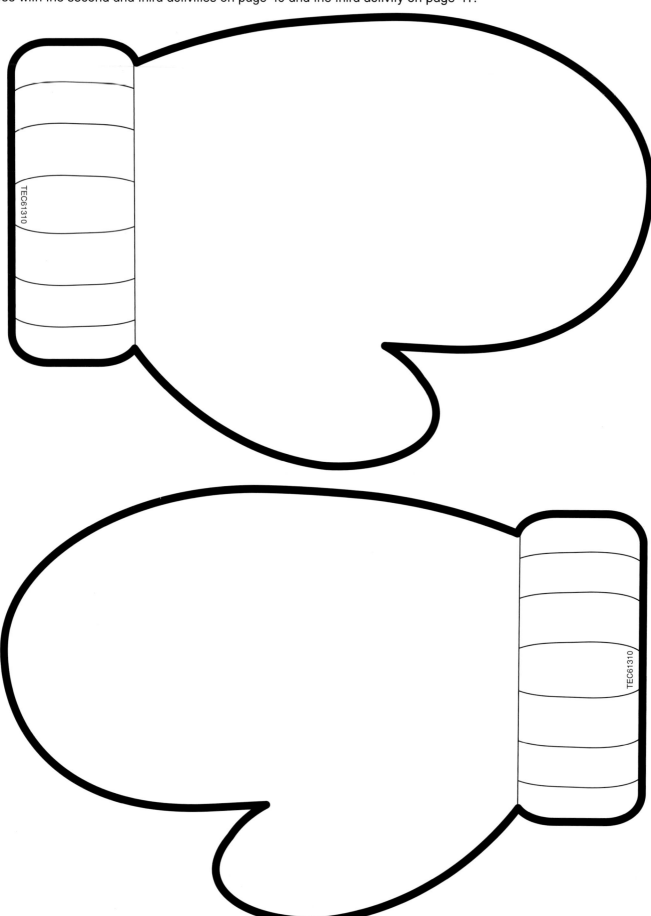

TEC61310

Thematic Fun for Little Learners • ©The Mailbox® Books • TEC61310

Name _____

Mouse-Made Mittens

Color.

Note to the teacher: Have a child color the matching mittens in each row.

43

Dental Health

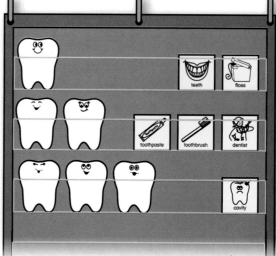

Literacy: Cut out a copy of the dental health cards on page 46. Arrange tooth cutouts (patterns on page 47) in a pocket chart, as shown, to represent one-, two-, and three-syllable words. Hold up a card and have students name the picture. Discuss how the picture relates to dental health. Then have students clap the syllables in the word. Invite a child to place the card in the appropriate row. Continue with each remaining card.

Social studies: This idea reinforces healthy habits! Ask each child to pretend her index finger is a toothbrush. Have her squeeze imaginary toothpaste on her brush. Then have youngsters pretend to brush their teeth as you lead them in reciting the chant shown. For added fun, turn the lights off when you chant the word *night* and then on again when you chant *day.*

> Brush your teeth, brush your teeth
> Every morning.
> Brush your teeth, brush your teeth
> Every night.
> Brush your teeth, brush your teeth
> Every day.
> Brushing helps fight tooth decay!

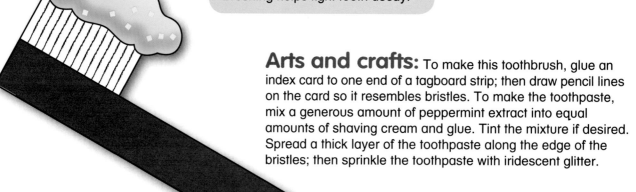

Arts and crafts: To make this toothbrush, glue an index card to one end of a tagboard strip; then draw pencil lines on the card so it resembles bristles. To make the toothpaste, mix a generous amount of peppermint extract into equal amounts of shaving cream and glue. Tint the mixture if desired. Spread a thick layer of the toothpaste along the edge of the bristles; then sprinkle the toothpaste with iridescent glitter.

Math: Label craft foam teeth with numbers from 1 to 10. If desired, program the back of each tooth with a matching dot set. Place the teeth beneath pillows and provide tooth fairy props, such as a wand, a crown, and wings. A youngster uses the props as desired and picks up each tooth. Then she places the teeth in numerical order. For an extra challenge, provide a greater number of teeth.

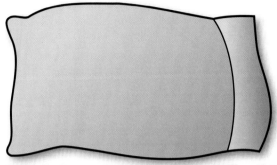

Song: If desired, make a simple tooth pointer. Then give the pointer (baton) to a child and have him use it to conduct a sing-along of this catchy song.

(sung to the tune of "Twinkle, Twinkle, Little Star")

Brush your teeth and floss them too.
Watch the types of food you chew.
Too much candy, gum, and cake
May give you a bad toothache.
Brush your teeth and floss them too.
Watch the types of food you chew.

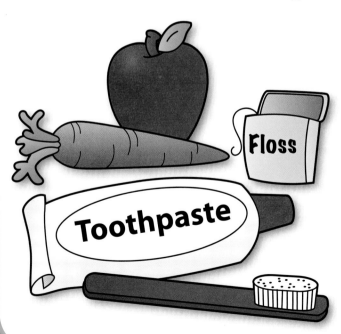

Social studies: Display items that promote dental health, such as toothpaste, a toothbrush, dental floss, an apple, and a carrot. Have little ones name each item and tell how it is related to healthy teeth. Lead them to understand that chewing crunchy foods like apples and carrots helps clean teeth (but that they should still brush after eating). Then have youngsters close their eyes. While their eyes are closed, remove one of the items. Have students open their eyes; then encourage a child to name the missing item. Repeat the activity several times, removing a different item each time.

Dental Health Cards

Use with the first activity on page 44.

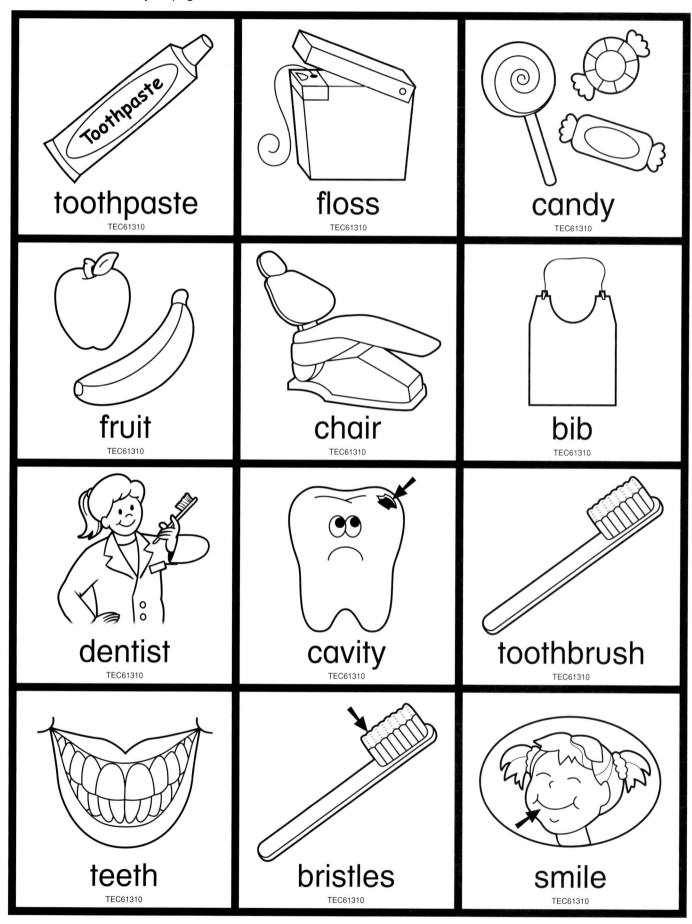

toothpaste
TEC61310

floss
TEC61310

candy
TEC61310

fruit
TEC61310

chair
TEC61310

bib
TEC61310

dentist
TEC61310

cavity
TEC61310

toothbrush
TEC61310

teeth
TEC61310

bristles
TEC61310

smile
TEC61310

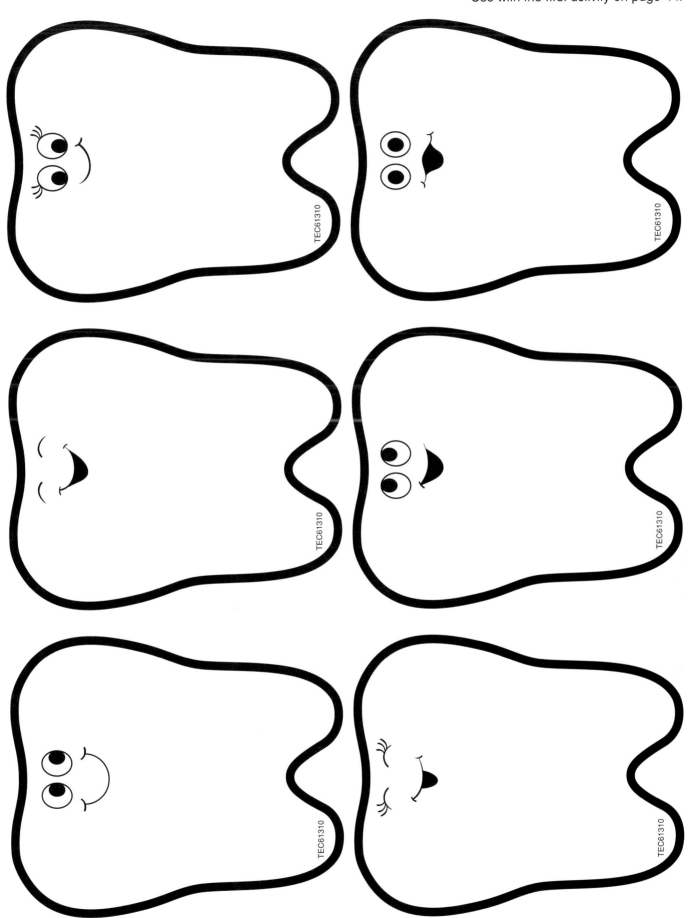

TEC61310

TEC61310

TEC61310

TEC61310

TEC61310

TEC61310

Groundhogs

Literacy: Youngsters will be fascinated to hear that groundhogs are also called whistle pigs because of the whistling sound they make. Place letter cards in your pocket chart. Place a small groundhog cutout (patterns on page 50) behind several of the cards. Have a child name a letter and then remove the card. If a groundhog is revealed, have students make their best whistling noise. Continue with each remaining card.

Math: Have a child (groundhog) curl up on the floor and pretend she is asleep in a burrow. Then lead the rest of the group in reciting the rhyme shown, prompting the groundhog to wake up and look around at the end of the countdown. Ask the groundhog whether she sees her shadow. If she does, say, "Oh no! Six more weeks of winter!" If she doesn't, say, "Yay! Spring is coming soon!" Then have the groundhog switch places with a classmate, who then becomes the groundhog.

> Furry little groundhog
> Sleeping underground,
> When you hear the number one,
> Wake up and look around.
> Ten, nine, eight, seven, six, five, four, three, two, one!

Arts and crafts: Enlarge the large groundhog pattern on page 50 and make a construction paper copy. Have a child paint the groundhog with brown paint. Then prompt her to drag a comb through the paint several times so it resembles a furry texture. When the paint is dry, cut out the groundhog.

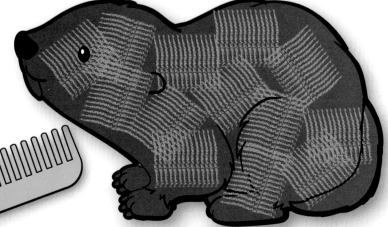

Science: To have youngsters explore shadows, show them a tagboard groundhog cutout (see the large groundhog pattern on page 50). Hold the cutout upright and have a child use a flashlight to shine a light on it, leading youngsters to notice the groundhog's shadow. For independent exploration, place the cutout, the flashlight, and a variety of classroom objects at a center. Encourage students to use the items to explore shadows.

Song: Have students pretend to emerge from a burrow and then sing the first verse of the song below, predicting six more weeks of winter. Then encourage them to repeat the process with the second verse, predicting the arrival of spring!

(sung to the tune of "Are You Sleeping?")

Where's that shadow?
Where's that shadow?
There it is!
There it is!
Six more weeks of winter.
Six more weeks of winter.
Brrrr, brrrr, brrrr!
Brrrr, brrrr, brrrr!

Where's that shadow?
Where's that shadow?
It's not here!
It's not here!
Spring will soon be coming.
Spring will soon be coming.
Nice and warm,
Nice and warm!

Fine motor: Youngsters place a groundhog's favorite items in its burrow! In advance, draw a simple burrow on a sheet of brown bulletin board paper. Attach a groundhog cutout (see the large groundhog pattern on page 50) to the burrow. Then place the paper at a center. To begin, explain to youngsters that groundhogs live in burrows, which are tunnels in the ground. Groundhogs like to put their favorite foods in their burrows. Encourage students to glue green paper shreds (grass), red pom-poms (berries), and torn pieces of paper (leaves) to the burrow.

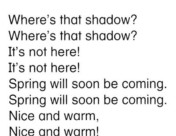

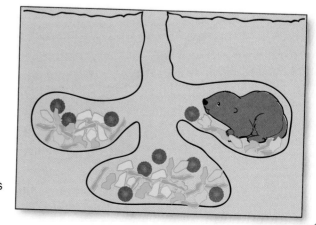

See page 51 for a reproducible activity!

Small Groundhog Patterns
Use with the first activity on page 48.

TEC61310

TEC61310

Large Groundhog Pattern
Use with the third activity on page 48 and the first and third activities on page 49.

TEC61310

Thematic Fun for Little Learners • ©The Mailbox® Books • TEC61310

Name _____

Where's That Shadow?

Thematic Fun for Little Learners • ©The Mailbox® Books • TEC61310

Note to the teacher: Have a youngster color a copy of the page. Then have him glue squares of black tissue paper behind the groundhog to show its shadow.

Hearts

Math: Conceal a number card in a heart-shaped box. Direct youngsters to pass the heart around the circle as you lead them in singing the song shown. At the end of the song, signal youngsters to stop. Then have the child with the box remove the lid and show the card to the group. Encourage youngsters to identify the number; then replace the card with a different number card and begin again.

(sung to the tune of "If You're Happy and You Know It")

There's a number in the heart; yes, there is!
There's a number in the heart; yes, there is!
Oh, what could that number be?
Maybe two or ten or three?
There's a number in the heart; yes, there is!

Literacy: Place a heart cutout on the floor in front of each child. Have youngsters say the word *heart* and practice its beginning sound. Then tell little ones to listen carefully as you announce a word. If the word begins with /h/ like *heart,* students hop over their heart cutouts. If the word begins with a different sound, youngsters stand still. Continue the activity with other words that begin with /h/ and some that do not.

Arts and crafts: To make this lovely artwork, spritz water over heart-shaped pieces of newsprint and smooth them onto a sheet of fingerpainting paper. The hearts will stick to the paper! Fingerpaint over the entire paper. Then remove the hearts. What a lovely masterpiece!

See page 55 for a reproducible activity!

Math: Cut out a class supply of hearts in three different colors and place them around the room. Also display a three-column graph like the one shown. Send little ones on a heart hunt. When each child returns with one heart, help her place it in the appropriate column on the graph. After all the hearts are in place, lead students in counting the number of hearts in each column. Then help youngsters compare the results, using words such as *more, fewer,* or e*qual.*

Song: Encourage little ones to run in place. After a few moments, have each child put her hand on her chest to feel her heartbeat. Then lead youngsters in the rhyme shown, prompting each child to pat her chest when she says "dub, dub, dub, dub, dub" and circle her finger in the air during "whoo, whoo, whoo!" Repeat the activity, inserting other students' names in the rhyme.

[Sarah] has a heart, and it goes like this: dub, dub, dub, dub, dub!
[Sarah] has a heart, and it goes like this: dub, dub, dub, dub, dub!
It doesn't go crash or bang or moo.
It doesn't go crunch or whoo, whoo, whoo!
[Sarah] has a heart, and it goes like this: dub, dub, dub, dub, dub!

Literacy: Cut out a copy of the cards on page 54 and place them in a gift bag. Invite a child to take a card from the bag. Lead the rest of the group in the chant shown. At the end of the chant, have the student display the card and identify the picture. Encourage youngsters to clap the syllables in the word and then identify the number of claps. Set the card aside and continue until the bag is empty.

Please, tell us what is on the heart,
So we can clap the word apart!

Picture Cards

Use with the third activity on page 53.

TEC61310

TEC61310

TEC61310

TEC61310

TEC61310

TEC61310

TEC61310

TEC61310

TEC61310

Hippo's Hearts

Note to the teacher: Have a child trace each balloon. Have her squeeze glue along each balloon string and then press three-inch lengths of string or yarn on the glue.

Post Office

Literacy: To prepare for this listening and speaking activity, pack a few familiar items in a box. Then label the box with your school name, address, and a mock return address. Tell little ones the package arrived in the mail. Focus their attention on the addresses and explain why the information is important. Then open the box with great fanfare! Give youngsters clues to help them guess one of the items. When the item is guessed, remove it from the box and set it aside. Continue until the package is empty.

Literacy: Write letters on a class supply of papers and stuff each one in an envelope. Place the envelopes in a tote bag (mailbag). Give the mailbag to a youngster (postal worker). Have her choose a classmate and say, "I have a letter for [classmate's name]!" Encourage the child to give an envelope to the child. Then prompt the child to open the envelope and say, "My letter is [letter name]." Continue with each remaining child.

Arts and crafts: To make this personalized postal craft, help a child write his name and address on a mailbox cutout (pattern on page 58). Invite him to draw designs on the mailbox and decorate it with stickers. Have him glue a brown paper strip (post) to the back of the mailbox; then help him attach a red flag cutout to the mailbox using a brad.

Literacy: Cut apart a copy of the cards on page 59. Put each card in a separate envelope marked with the first letter of the picture's name. Each day, put a different envelope in a classroom mailbox. During group time, have a child remove the envelope and give it to you. Have youngsters identify the letter and its sound. Then help them brainstorm words that begin with that sound. After naming several words, prompt the child to remove the "mail" from the envelope so students can see whether the picture on the card matches one of the words they suggested.

Song: Lead little ones in singing this cute song. Then invite youngsters to discuss letters or any other mail—such as a package, a postcard, or a children's magazine—they may have received.

(sung to the tune of "Did You Ever See a Lassie?")

Did you ever get a letter, a letter, a letter?
Did you ever get a letter that came in the mail?
Oh, who sent that letter? Oh, who sent that letter?
Did you ever get a letter that came in the mail?

Math: Put an assortment of mail—such as packages, letters, and magazines—in a container labeled "Mail Bin." Label separate containers for each type of mail and place a corresponding item in each container. A child pretends to be a postal worker sorting the mail. She removes a piece of mail from the mail bin and places it in the appropriate container. She continues until all the mail is sorted.

Mailbox Pattern
Use with the third activity on page 56.

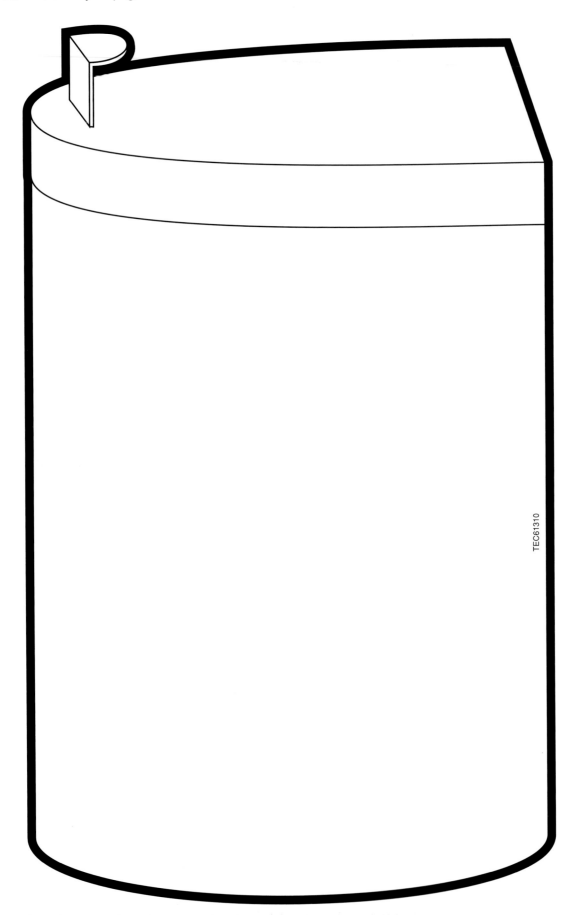

TEC61310

TEC61310

TEC61310

TEC61310

TEC61310

TEC61310

TEC61310

TEC61310

TEC61310

TEC61310

TEC61310

TEC61310

TEC61310

Dr. Seuss

Literacy: After sharing the classic story *The Cat in the Hat,* ask students whether the cat's ideas for rainy day fun were good or bad. After youngsters explain their thoughts, walk around the group and drop a tagboard raindrop on a child's lap. Have him say, "On a rainy day, I would…" and encourage him to name something fun or helpful he would do. Then have that child walk around the group and drop the raindrop on a classmate's lap. Continue for several rounds.

Math: After a read-aloud of *The Foot Book,* invite several children to stand in front of the group. Lead the class in reciting the rhyme shown and counting the students' feet. Then prompt youngsters to say, "I meet [number] feet," encouraging them to name the total number of feet counted. Repeat the activity several times, inviting different numbers of children to have their feet counted each time.

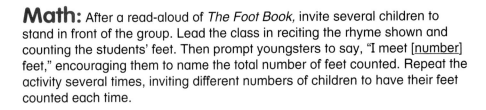

I see many, many feet!
Let's all count the feet we meet.

Arts and crafts: In advance, gather yellow craft feathers (Sneech feathers) and place them at a table with shallow pans of yellow paint. Read aloud the story "The Sneeches" from the book *The Sneeches and Other Stories.* Then bring a small group of youngsters to the table and give each child a Sneech feather. Encourage her to use her feather to paint a sheet of paper as desired. When the paint is dry, have her attach red star stickers to the page—just like the stars on the Sneeches' bellies!

See page 63 for a reproducible activity!

Literacy: Cut apart a copy of the rhyming cards on page 62. After a read-aloud of *Hop on Pop,* display one card from each pair in a pocket chart. Stack the remaining cards several feet away. Invite a child to take a card from the stack and say the picture's name. Have her hop to the chart as the group chants, "Hop, pop, stop!" Then have her place her card beside the rhyming card. Finally, say, "Rhyme, rhyme, what is this rhyme?" prompting the group to chant, "[Mouse], [house]!" Repeat the activity with each remaining card.

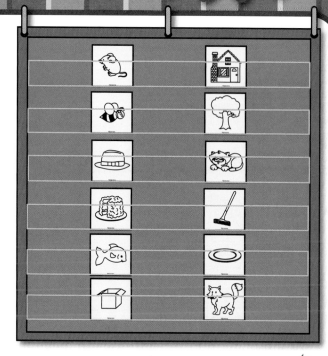

Song: After reading aloud the Dr. Seuss classic *Green Eggs and Ham,* engage little ones in singing this silly song and naming other rhyming pairs from the story.

(sung to the tune of "Are You Sleeping?")

I am Sam. I am Sam.
Sam-I-am. Sam-I-am.
Would you like some green ham—
Tasty eggs and green ham—
With a [fox] and a [box]?

Math: Cut out an even number of fish in different colors (patterns on page 106). Attach a jumbo paper clip to each fish and place it on a sheet of blue paper (ocean). After a read-aloud of *One Fish, Two Fish, Red Fish, Blue Fish,* choose two children and give them a magnetic fishing pole. After each child in the pair catches a fish, have the group chant, "One fish, two fish, [orange] fish, [black] fish," prompting students to insert the color names of the two fish. Then set the two fish aside. Repeat the activity with new fishermen.

Rhyming Cards

Use with the first activity on page 61.

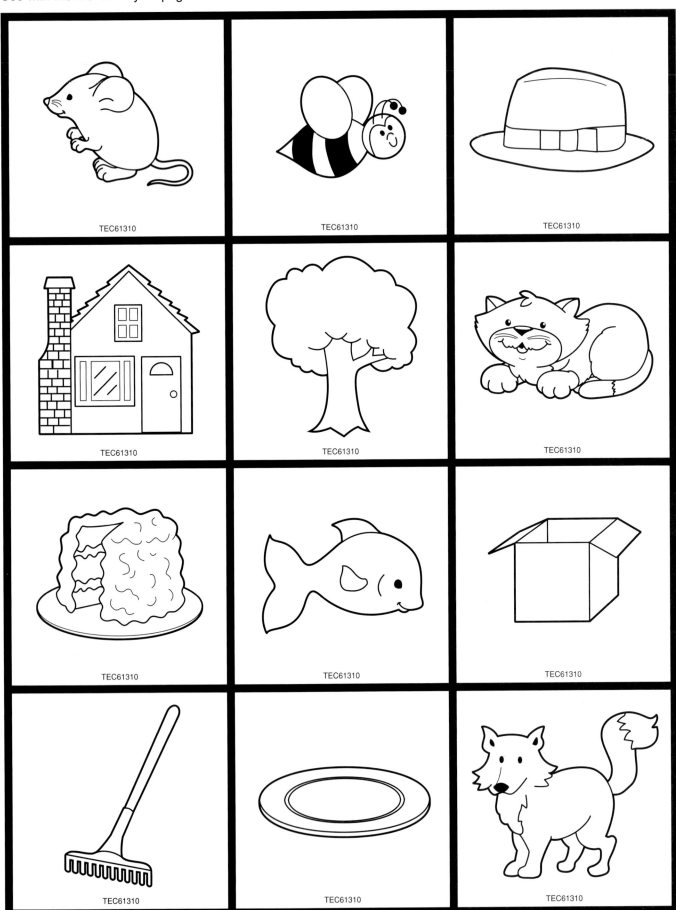

TEC61310

TEC61310

TEC61310

TEC61310

TEC61310

TEC61310

TEC61310

TEC61310

TEC61310

TEC61310

TEC61310

TEC61310

Thematic Fun for Little Learners • ©The Mailbox® Books • TEC61310

Name

Green Gourmet

Thematic Fun for Little Learners • ©The Mailbox® Books • TEC61310

Note to the teacher: Have each child color the utensils and plate on a copy of this page. Then encourage her to glue green tissue paper squares to the eggs and ham.

Shamrocks and Leprechauns

Math: Display several leprechaun cutouts (pattern on page 66) around the room so their locations encourage the use of positional words. For example, you might put a leprechaun *under* a chair, *beside* the clock, *above* the door, *on* a windowsill, *in* a basket, and *below* the calendar. Have a youngster walk around the room and search for the leprechauns. When he finds one, have him call out, "I spy a leprechaun!" Then prompt him to use a positional word to describe where the leprechaun is located.

Literacy: Have students say the word *leprechaun* and practice its beginning sound. Then encourage each child to perform her own version of a leprechaun jig. Tell your little leprechauns to listen carefully as you announce a word. If the word begins with /l/ like *leprechaun,* youngsters say, "/l/, /l/, /l/" and dance their leprechaun jigs. If the word begins with a different sound, students stand still.

Arts and crafts: Invite a child to put dollops of yellow and blue paint on a tray. Encourage her to use her fingertips or a paintbrush to blend the two colors. Next, have her place a shamrock cutout (enlarged copy of the pattern on page 66) atop the paint, gently rub her hand across the shamrock, and then remove the shamrock from the tray. Finally, have her sprinkle iridescent glitter (leprechaun dust) on the wet paint.

Literacy: Write the chant shown on sentence strips, leaving a space in place of the initial consonant in the final word. Place the strips in your pocket chart. Gather several consonant cards and place them nearby. Also put a letter *g* card aside. Explain that you have a chant for students to learn but you can't remember the last word. Have a child choose a letter and place it in the chart as shown. (Allow real words and nonsense words.) Have students help you read the chant. When the giggles die down, exclaim, "No, that's not right!" Continue with each remaining card. Then say, "I remember! The word is supposed to be *gold*." Reveal the correct card and place it in the chart. Then have students recite the chant correctly.

Oh, leprechaun, leprechaun, I am told

That you have a pot of [m]old.

Song: Encourage students to sing this catchy little leprechaun song!

(sung to the tune of "If You're Happy and You Know It")

If you find that you should meet a leprechaun,
If you find that you should meet a leprechaun,
He may say, "Top o' the morning,"
And then, without any warning,
He is gone, and there is no more leprechaun!

Name _____   Syllables _____

Lucky's Pot of Gold!

Thematic Fun for Little Learners • ©The Mailbox® Books • TEC61310

Literacy: Give each child a copy of page 67 and ten Ritz Bits cracker sandwiches (gold coins). Announce one of the following words: *green, gold, rainbow, pot, shamrock,* or *leprechaun.* Encourage youngsters to clap once for each syllable they hear and then identify the number of syllables. After confirming that the number of syllables is correct, have each student place that many crackers on her pot. Repeat the activity with the remaining words. After each child's pot is filled with her edible coins, invite her to snack on them!

Leprechaun Pattern
Use with the first activity on page 64.

Shamrock Pattern
Use with the third activity on page 64.

Name _____

Lucky's Pot of Gold!

Note to the teacher: Use with the third idea on page 65.

Math: Cut apart a few copies of the bunny cards on page 70. Add grass details to a length of green paper (meadow); then place the meadow on the floor. Place cards to make an *ABC* pattern. Then prompt students to use the extra cards to extend the pattern. Repeat the process with other patterns.

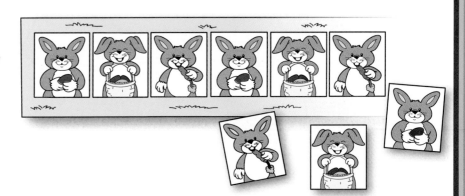

Science: Partially fill several pairs of plastic eggs with a dry substance—such as rice, beans, or pennies—and then secure the halves together with tape. Provide a sterilized foam egg carton and a bunny headband (ear patterns on page 71). A child puts on the headband and chooses an egg. He shakes the egg and uses his bunny ears to listen to the sound. Then he shakes each remaining egg, in turn, to find the matching sound. When he finds the matching sound, he puts the pair of eggs in the egg carton. He continues until all the eggs are paired.

Arts and crafts: To make this multicolored egg art, place an egg-shaped cutout in a lidded plastic box. Dip marbles in paint, place them in the box, and then secure the lid. Tilt and shake the box. Then remove the lid and remove the marbles to reveal this egg masterpiece.

Gross motor: Label several paper strips with directions such as "Rub your tummy and then touch your toes." Put each strip in a plastic egg and put the eggs in a basket. To play, a student (bunny) hops around the circle carrying the basket as you lead the group in the chant shown. At the end of the chant, the bunny stops and hands an egg to the child closest to him. That child removes the strip from the egg for an adult to read aloud. After the group performs the actions, the youngsters switch places. Play continues until the basket is empty.

Little bunny, hop, hop, hop!
Now it's time for you to stop!

Rub your tummy and then touch your toes.

Song: Scatter plastic vegetables on the floor so they resemble a garden. Invite a few youngsters (bunnies) to hop around the garden, pretending to munch on the veggies as you lead the rest of the group in singing the song shown. Repeat the song several times so all your little bunnies get a turn in the garden!

(sung to the tune of "My Bonnie Lies Over the Ocean")

The bunnies will hop through the garden.
They eat all the carrots and greens.
They munch on the lettuce and cabbage
And chew on the peas and green beans.
Munching, munching, the bunnies will eat all the veggies there.
Munching, munching, and that garden plot will be bare!

Bunny, funny.

Literacy: Invite youngsters to pretend to be bunnies resting in the grass. Tell your little bunnies to listen carefully for rhyming words. Then say the word *bunny* along with another word (real or nonsense). If the words rhyme, each little bunny hops up and down. If the words do not rhyme, the bunnies rest quietly in the grass. Continue with other word pairs.

Bunny Cards

Use with the first activity on page 68.

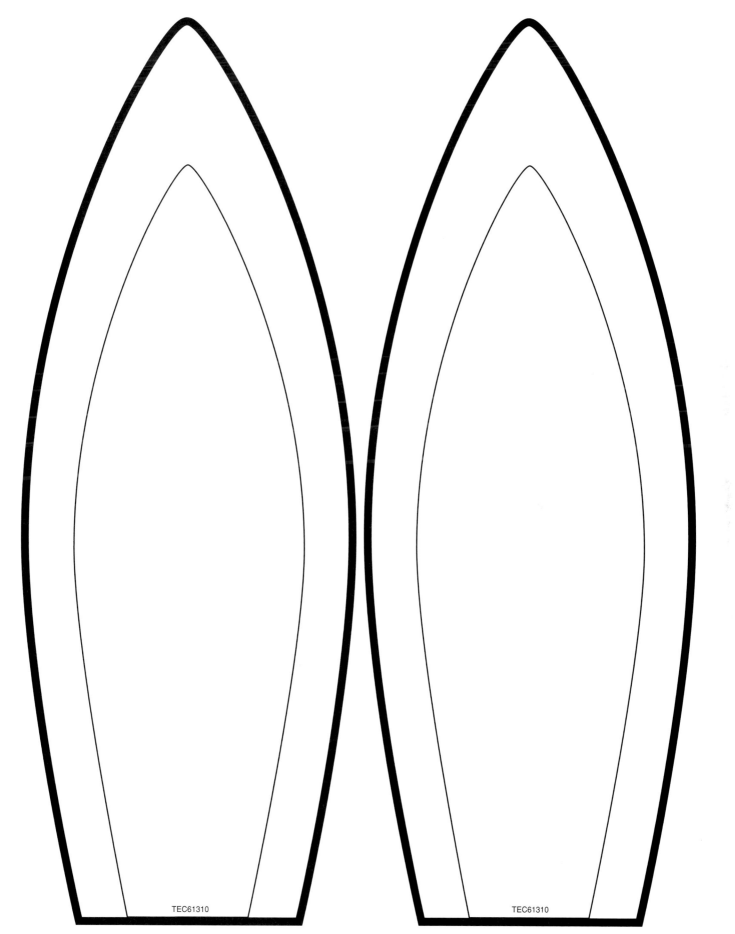

TEC61310

TEC61310

Thematic Fun for Little Learners • ©The Mailbox® Books • TEC61310

Note to the teacher: Use with the second activity on page 68. To make an adjustable headband, staple or glue two bunny ear cutouts to a tagboard strip. Then attach a length of self-adhesive Velcro fastener to each end of the strip.

Spring Weather

Literacy: Youngsters sequence clouds for this cute accordion booklet! Accordion-fold a 6" x 18" piece of paper for each child. Have each child cut out the cloud cards from a copy of page 74. Then encourage her to sequence the clouds from lightest to darkest. After checking the order, have her glue the cards to her booklet. Then she glues tinsel strands (or iridescent blue shreds) to the final cloud so they resemble rain.

Math: Use a pencil or similar object to gently tap a surface, simulating the sound of falling raindrops. Ask youngsters to silently count as you tap; then have students tell how many raindrops fell. After the correct number is given, prompt little ones to pat their legs that many times, counting aloud as they pat. Repeat the activity several times.

Snack: To make a cloud puff, help a child put one-fourth cup of marshmallow cream and one-fourth cup of powdered milk in a disposable bowl. Encourage her to work the ingredients with a fork until a soft dough forms. Then have her place the dough on a disposable plate and mold it into different cloud shapes. After reshaping the dough several times, invite her to eat her cloud-shaped snack!

See page 75 for a reproducible activity!

Math: Put a supply of blue linking cubes (raindrops) in two separate bags. Post two cloud-shaped cutouts on a wall several feet apart. Invite a pair of students to each take a bag and stand near a different cloud. Direct each child to take a handful of raindrops from his bag, hold them near his cloud, and let them go. Help each youngster count aloud the raindrops that fell from his cloud; then lead the group in comparing the results, using words such as *more, fewer,* and *equal.*

Song: Dripping raindrops, breezy trees, thunder crashing, puddle splashing! This cute action song is sure to remind your youngsters of spring!

(sung to the tune of "Are You Sleeping?")

Dripping raindrops, dripping raindrops,
There's a breeze through the trees.
I know that it's springtime.
Yes, it must be springtime—
Thunder, crash; puddle, splash!

Pat hands on thighs.
Wave arms to and fro.
Shake finger.
Shake finger.
Clap hands; stomp feet.

Science: Elicit a discussion about wind, leading youngsters to name things they have seen blow in the wind. Then display a tray containing several items that will blow in the wind and some that will not. Ask students to predict which items will blow in the wind and which ones will not and explain why. To test their predictions, point a blow-dryer toward the tray and turn it on; then compare youngsters' predictions to the actual results. To further the investigation, use the various dryer settings to see whether the wind strength affects the results.

Cloud Cards

Use with the first activity on page 72.

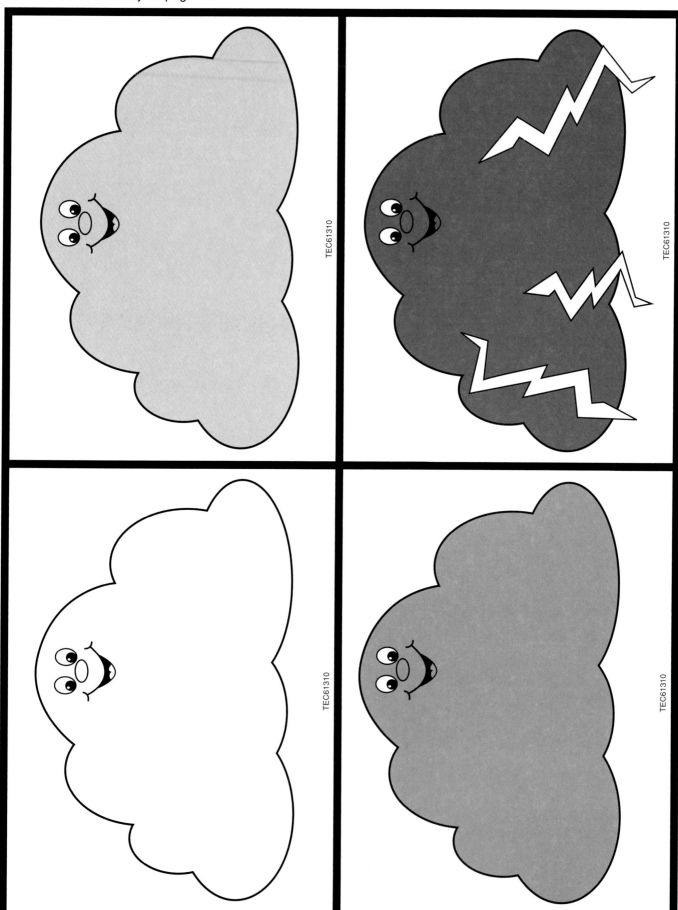

Thematic Fun for Little Learners • ©The Mailbox® Books • TEC61310

Windy Day

Thematic Fun for Little Learners • ©The Mailbox® Books • TEC61310

Note to the teacher: Help each child cut out the cards at the bottom of the page. Then, in each box, have her glue a card picturing an item that blows in the wind.

Pond

Math: Cut out multiple green construction paper copies of the frog cards on page 78. Also cut a large and a small log shape from brown paper. Scatter the frogs around the logs. Invite a child to pick a frog, identify it as a big frog or little frog, and then "hop" the frog to the matching log. Invite the rest of the class to join you in saying the following chant.

> You picked a [big] frog!
> Please put the [big] frog on the [big] log.

Science: To inform little ones that some pond animals hatch from eggs, ask each child to curl into a ball and pretend to be an egg. Recite the rhyme and name an appropriate pond animal—such as a tadpole, duckling, fish, turtle, or snake. Each youngster "hatches" and mimics the movements of the named animal.

> I see a little egg. It's at the pond.
> It's ready to hatch. It won't be long.
> What's inside? Soon we'll know.
> Wow! It's a [duckling]! Watch it go!

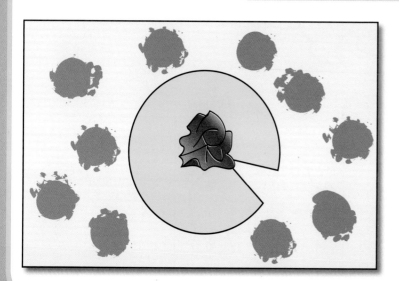

Arts and crafts: For this splashy process art, have a youngster dip a toy hammer into dark blue paint. Encourage her to gently tap her hammer on a sheet of light blue paper, saying "Splash!" each time she does so. If desired, have her add a lily pad cutout (pattern on page 78) with a tissue paper lily to her artwork.

See page 79 for a reproducible activity!

Math: For this partner center, provide two paper plate frogs like the ones shown, a bowl of black pompoms (flies), and a large foam die. Each child takes a frog. In turn, each partner rolls the die and places the matching number of flies on his frog. Then the partners compare their sets of flies using the words *more, fewer,* or *the same.*

Song: Little ones will enjoy acting like pond critters when they sing this fun action song!

(sung to the tune of "If You're Happy and You Know It")

Oh, the little [fishies swim] around the pond.
Oh, the little [fishies swim] around the pond.
Yes, they are very, very fond
Of the splishy, splashy pond.
Oh, the little [fishies swim] around the pond.

Continue with the following: froggies hop, dragonflies buzz, turtles sit, duckies fly

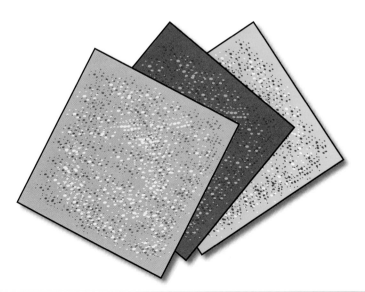

 Gross motor: Ask little ones to hop like frogs to and from center activities and to group time. To have youngsters imitate turtles, put two or three carpet squares or foam boards (shells) at your gross-motor center. Invite little ones to practice crawling around the room with the shells on their backs!

Frog Cards
Use with the first activity on page 76.

TEC61310

TEC61310

Lily Pad Pattern
Use with the third activity on page 76.

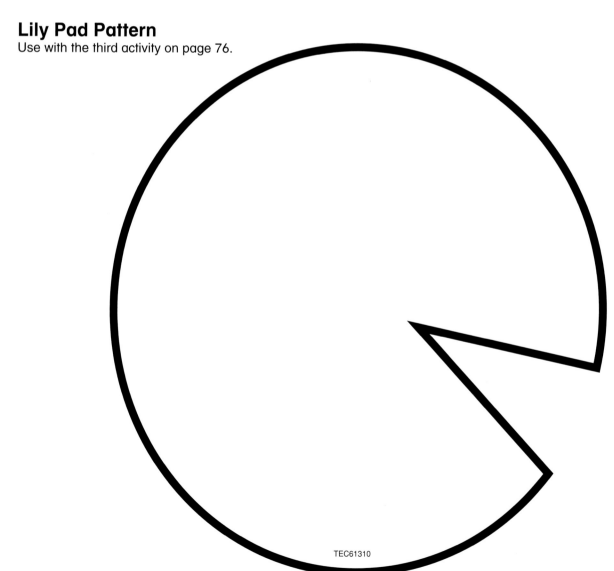

TEC61310

A Swell Shell

Thematic Fun for Little Learners • ©The Mailbox® Books • TEC61310

Note to the teacher: Have students tear different shades of green construction paper scraps and glue them to the turtle's shell.

Birds

Fine motor: Provide play dough, twigs, feathers, leaves, and yarn. If desired, attach bird cutouts to craft sticks (bird pattern on page 82). A child molds play dough into a nest shape. Then he adds items to the play dough so it resembles a real nest. Finally, he pushes a bird cutout into the nest.

Literacy: Have students sit in a circle. Then have a volunteer (robin) sit in the middle of the circle in a plastic hoop (nest). Tell students that the robin is a bird that has a red chest. Then explain that this particular bird wants things in her nest that begin with /b/. Recite the chant shown, prompting the robin to agree that she would like a ball in her nest because *ball* begins with /b/. Continue with different youngsters and words (see suggestions shown).

> Little robin red breast,
> Would you like a [ball] in your nest?

Continue with the following: *bat, bear, book, cake, box, bell, horse, bow, jeep, bus, balloon, bowl, boot, ring, boat, bag, mouse*

Arts and crafts: This process art is a fun sensory project! Give each child cold spaghetti noodles on a colorful paper plate. Encourage him to touch the noodles, swirl them around, and arrange them as desired. Then have him attach a bird cutout (pattern on page 82) to the edge of the plate. When the noodles dry, they remain attached to the paper plate. Now that bird has a plate full of worms!

See page 83 for a reproducible activity!

Math: Make a large yarn circle (bird nest) on the floor. Invite a student (bird) to "fly" around the room and land in the nest. Then lead the group in the rhyme shown. During the last line, prompt one more bird to fly around the room and land in the nest. Then lead students in counting the total number of birds in the nest. Repeat the activity several times, inserting appropriate numbers and pronouns until the nest is full. Then announce that all the birds are home!

[One] little bird(s) sat in a nest
Wondering, "Where are all the rest?"
[It] said, "Tweet, tweet, [I'm] all alone!"
Then one more bird came flying back home.

Song: Encourage youngsters to make up motions for each verse of this catchy song!

(sung to the tune of "The Muffin Man")

Do you see the birdies fly,
The birdies fly, the birdies fly?
Do you see the birdies fly
So high up in the sky?

Continue with the following: *Do you hear the birdies tweet/When all the birdies meet; Do you see the birdies feed/On tasty birdie seed*

Math: Cut out several copies of the bird and nest patterns on page 82. Label each bird with a different number. Program each nest with a corresponding number of sticky dots (eggs). Invite a child to choose a nest and count the eggs aloud. Then encourage her to find the bird with that number and "fly" it to the nest. Continue until each bird is in its correct nest.

Bird Pattern

Use with the first and third activities on page 80 and the third activity on page 81.

Bird Nest Pattern

Use with the third activity on page 81.

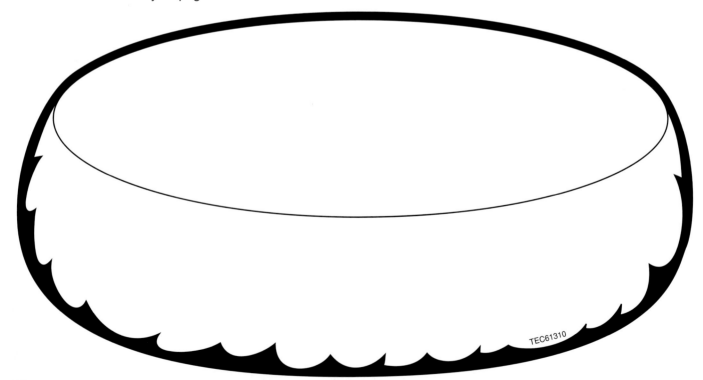

Name _____

Nests Full of Eggs

Cut.

Glue.

6

2

5

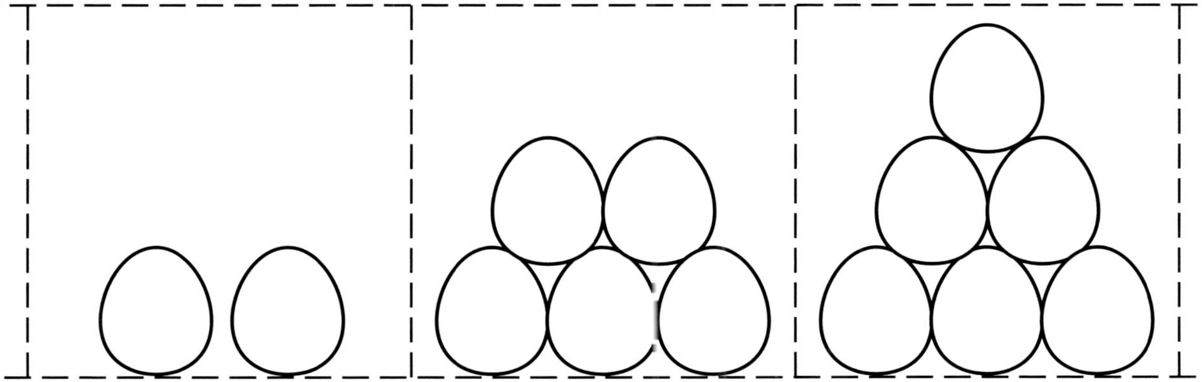

Note to the teacher: Help each child cut out the cards at the bottom of the page. Have him count the eggs on each card and then glue it above the nest with that number.

Flowers

Literacy: Cut out a copy of the flower growth cards on page 86 and place them facedown on the floor (making sure the cards are out of sequence). Invite volunteers, in turn, to flip over a card and describe the picture. After all the cards are faceup, guide the group to notice that the pictures are not in the correct order. Have students help you arrange the cards in the proper order; then invite youngsters to "read" the picture sequence to explain how a flower grows.

 **Science:** Talk about things a flower needs to grow, such as water and sunlight. Then have each child kneel on the floor and pretend to be a tiny flower. Dim the lights and lead little ones in singing the song shown. At the end of the first verse, pretend to water your tiny flowers, prompting them to rise to their knees as if they were growing. At the end of the second verse, turn on the lights, prompting your little flowers to "grow" big and tall.

(sung to the tune of "Are You Sleeping?")

Little flowers, little flowers,
Will you grow? Will you grow?
With a little water, with a little water,
Flowers grow! Flowers grow!

Little flowers, little flowers,
Will you grow? Will you grow?
With a little sunshine, with a little sunshine,
Flowers grow! Flowers grow!

Math: Place a pie tin filled with yellow pom-poms (pollen grains) atop a large flower-shaped cutout. A few feet from the flower, place several beehive cutouts (pattern on page 87), each labeled with a different number. Invite a child (bee) to identify the number on one of the hives. Then have the bee "fly" to the flower and count aloud that many pollen grains. Encourage the remaining youngsters to count along. Once the bee has collected the appropriate number of pollen grains, have her fly back and place them on the hive. Continue with each remaining beehive.

Arts and crafts: Provide shallow containers of paint and place an artificial flower next to each container. A child dips a flower in the paint and then uses it to paint on a sheet of paper as desired. She repeats the process with other flowers and paint colors.

Song: Give each of several children a different-colored flower cutout (pattern on page 87) and have them crouch on the floor. Prompt them to slowly rise to their feet as you lead the rest of the class in singing this simple song. At the end of the song, encourage students to name each flower's color.

(sung to the tune of "Are You Sleeping?")

See the flowers, see the flowers
Growing tall, growing tall.
There are many colors; there are many colors.
Name them all; name them all.

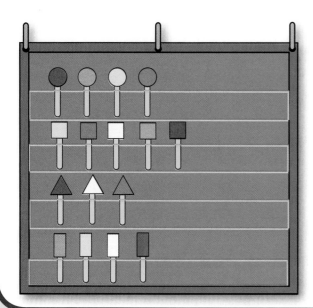

Math: Attach self-adhesive craft foam shapes to green craft sticks so they resemble flowers. Give each child a flower. Then sing the song shown, prompting students with the designated shape to hold their flowers in the air. After scanning for accuracy, have youngsters place the flowers in the same row of a pocket chart. Continue in the same way, encouraging youngsters who have already put their flowers in the chart to join you in singing the song.

(sung to the tune of "If You're Happy and You Know It")

If your flower is a [square], hold it up.
If your flower is a [square], hold it up.
Oh, I see flowers everywhere,
Flower shapes are here and there,
If your flower is a [square], hold it up!

Flower Growth Sequencing Cards

Use with the first activity on page 84.

Thematic Fun for Little Learners • ©The Mailbox® Books • TEC61310

Beehive Pattern
Use with the third activity on page 84.

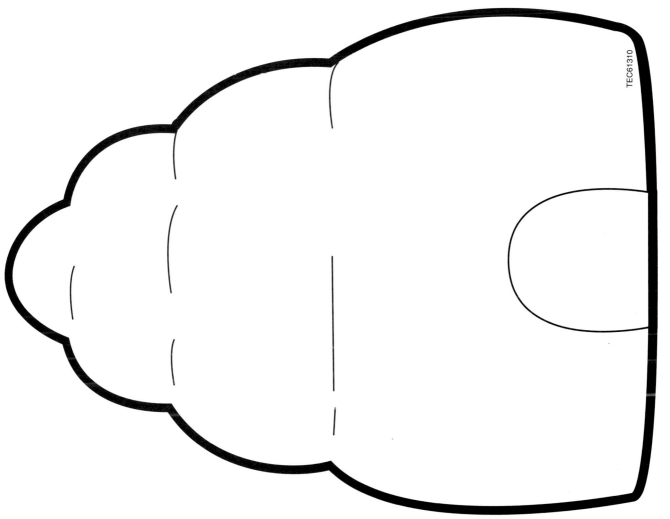

TEC61310

Flower Patterns
Use with the second idea on page 85, the first idea on page 89, and the third idea on page 113.

TEC61310

TEC61310

Butterflies

Math: To prepare for this partner activity, set out a copy of the large butterfly pattern on page 90, a set of number cards, and a supply of pom-poms. Instruct each child to take a card, read the number, and place that number of pom-poms on one of the butterfly's wings. Then have the pair determine which wing has more pom-poms on it. Direct the students to remove the pom-poms and play another round.

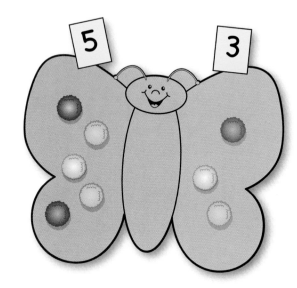

Song: Encourage youngsters to pretend to be beautiful butterflies while you lead them in singing this jaunty number.

(sung to the tune of "My Bonnie Lies Over the Ocean")

The butterflies fly through the meadow.
They fly to the flowers so bright.
They take all the sweet, tasty nectar.
Oh, they're such a colorful sight.
Flying, flying, they fly to the flowers so bright, so bright.
Flying, flying—oh, they're such a colorful sight!

Fine motor: Here's a simple idea that results in a beautiful butterfly craft. Give each child a heart cutout (wings), a craft stick with a face drawn on it (butterfly body), and access to colorful paper scraps and glue. Have her spread glue on the wings and cover the glue with torn paper pieces. Then have her glue the body to the center of the wings.

Math: Scatter a supply of colorful flower cutouts (enlarge the patterns on page 87) on the floor. Play a recording of lively music and prompt youngsters to pretend they are butterflies. Have students "fly" around the flowers. Then stop the music and announce a color. Direct the little butterflies to fly to a flower of that color and stand near it. Then start the music again to play another round.

Literacy: Write capital letters on your board, including several *B*s. Prompt a youngster to "fly" to the board, circle a letter *B*, and say, "/b/, /b/, butterfly!" Continue in the same way until all the *B*s are circled.

Literacy: Cut out ten butterfly cards (patterns on page 90) and cut out a copy of the picture cards on page 91. Place the picture cards in a pocket chart. Give each butterfly card to a different child. Prompt each child, in turn, to "fly" her butterfly to the chart and place it over a picture with a name that begins with /b/ like *butterfly*. Continue with each remaining butterfly. Then have students say the names of the uncovered pictures, noting that they do not begin with /b/.

Butterfly Pattern

Use with the first activity on page 88.

TEC61310

Butterfly Cards

Use with the third activity on page 89.

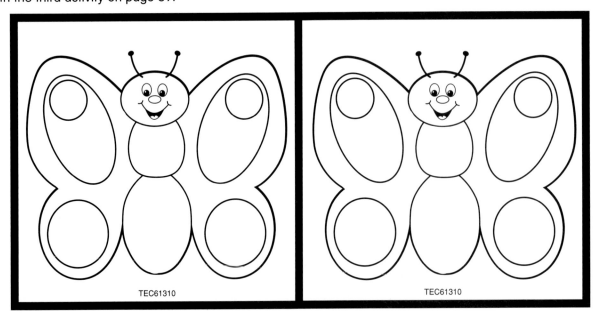

TEC61310   TEC61310

Thematic Fun for Little Learners • ©The Mailbox® Books • TEC61310

TEC61310

TEC61310

TEC61310

TEC61310

TEC61310

TEC61310

TEC61310

TEC61310

TEC61310

TEC61310

TEC61310

TEC61310

Picnic

Fine motor: Set out brown play dough, a cookie sheet (grill), a spatula, and several small disposable plates. A little cook molds the play dough to make hamburgers. Then she places them on the grill. When she thinks the hamburgers are cooked, she uses the spatula to put a hamburger on each plate.

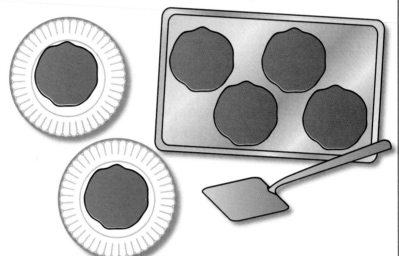

Song: Get little ones excited about the picnic season with this tune.

(sung to the tune of "Clementine")

Packed a picnic,
Packed a picnic,
Packed a picnic—I can't wait
To put hot dogs, to put carrots,
To put cookies on my plate!

Critical thinking: Place in a picnic basket items that are needed for a picnic along with a few items that are not. Bring the basket to the circle-time area, pretending that it is very heavy. Ask the group to help you make sure that you only packed the things needed for a picnic. Remove an item from the basket. Ask a volunteer to name the item; then guide the group to decide whether it is needed for a picnic. Continue with the remaining items.

See page 95 for a reproducible activity!

Arts and crafts:

To prepare for this watermelon-slice craft, set out pink paper semicircles, green tissue paper squares, glue, and a black ink pad. Have a child crumple tissue paper squares and glue them to the outer edge of the half circle so they resemble a rind. Then direct her to add several thumbprint seeds to the watermelon slice. If desired, invite the child to use decorative scissors to cut a bite from the slice.

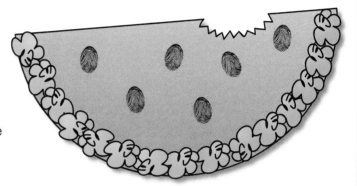

Math:

Give each child in a small group a sheet of decorative scrapbooking paper that resembles a picnic blanket (or red construction paper) and a black pom-pom (ant). Announce a direction such as "Place the ant on the blanket." Prompt each youngster to place his ant accordingly. Continue in this manner, using a different positional word each time.

Literacy:

Color and cut apart a copy of the food cards on page 94. Place the facedown stack of cards and a picnic basket in the circle-time area. Tell little ones that you are going on a picnic but only want to pack foods that begin with /p/. Invite a child to take a card and name the food. Then lead the group in saying the rhyme shown. Have the child decide whether the food name begins with /p/. If it does, prompt him to put the card in the basket. If not, have the child set the card aside. Continue with the remaining cards.

We're going on a picnic.
I hope you all can come!
Should we take [pumpkin]?
Yum, yum, yum!

Food Cards

Use with the third idea on page 93.

Thematic Fun for Little Learners • ©The Mailbox® Books • TEC61310

Picnic Favorites

Trace.

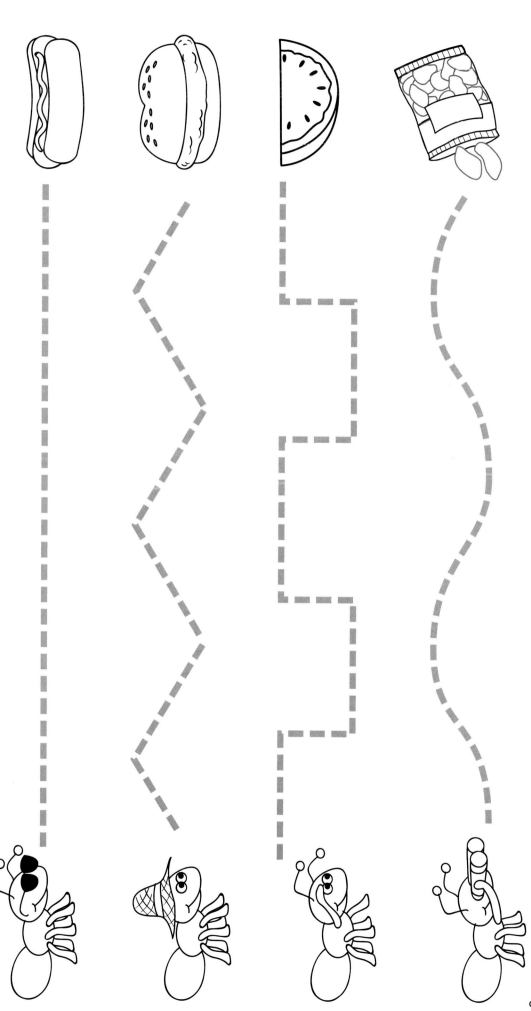

Ice Cream

Gross motor: Place a large bowl and a few ice cream scoopers in the center of a large open area. Scatter large pom-poms (ice cream scoops) around the bowl. Gather a few youngsters and tell them they are going to make a big ice cream sundae. Give each child an ice cream scooper and prompt her to scoop up the ice cream and plop it in the bowl. Continue until all the ice cream is in the bowl.

Song: After singing this sweet song with little ones, invite each child to name his favorite flavor of ice cream.

(sung to the tune of "Are You Sleeping?")

Let's eat ice cream, let's eat ice cream—
Smooth and sweet, smooth and sweet.
What's your favorite flavor, what's your favorite flavor?
What a treat, what a treat!

Science: This project focuses on the sense of touch! Have a child feel a piece of plastic canvas, noticing the bumpy texture. Place a cone cutout over the canvas and help the child use a brown crayon to make a rubbing on the cone. Attach the cone to a sheet of paper. Then paint the palm of the child's hand and have her make prints above the cone.

See page 99 for a reproducible activity!

Literacy: Write several letters on a supersize ice cream scoop cutout and place it on the floor. Place colorful manipulatives nearby. A child names a letter and then places a manipulative on top of it. When all the letters are covered, it looks like the ice cream scoop has candy sprinkles!

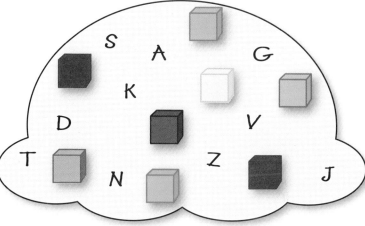

Math: Give each child in a small group a cone cutout and several large pom-poms (ice cream scoops). Write a number on a board and ask a volunteer to name the number. Lead the group in saying the chant shown, inserting the number where indicated. Then have each child place a matching number of scoops above her cone. After checking her work, direct her to remove the scoops to get ready for another round.

Ice cream, ice cream,
I shout with glee.
[Number] big scoops,
Just for me.

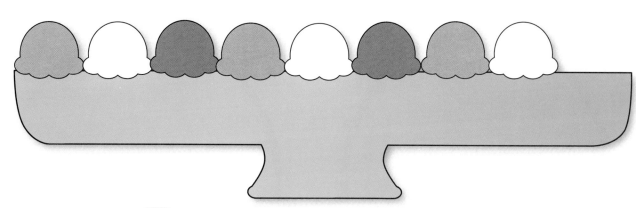

Math: Post an extremely long sundae bowl cutout on your tabletop. Place a supply of brown, pink, and white ice cream scoop cutouts (patterns on page 98) nearby. Prompt a student to arrange the scoops above the bowl to make a pattern. Then have her remove the scoops and make a new pattern.

Ice Cream Scoop Patterns

Use with the third activity on page 97.

TEC61310
TEC61310
TEC61310
TEC61310
TEC61310
TEC61310

Lots of Scoops

Color the 🍦 with **more.**

Color the 🍦 with **less.**

Snack: To make this edible beach, have each child spread blue-tinted frosting on a graham cracker. Direct her to sprinkle graham cracker crumbs on the lower half of the iced area. Finally, press a few bear-shaped crackers (beachgoers) into the frosting.

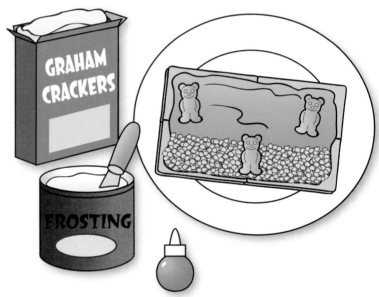

Math: Cut a towel or a piece of fabric into rectangles to make mini beach towels. Then set an equal number of mini beach towels and drink umbrellas near a sand table. A child arranges the beach towels in the sand. Then he sticks an umbrella in the sand near each towel.

Social studies: With this idea, youngsters identify with a real-life situation! In advance, hide a class supply of beach-themed items, such as empty sunscreen bottles, flip-flops, swimsuits, sunglasses, and beach towels. Show youngsters a large beach bag. Then tell them that you are packing for a trip to the beach and need their help to find all the things you need to take. Prompt each child to find one item you need for a beach trip. Invite him to name the item, explain how it would be useful on a beach trip, and place it in the beach bag.

See page 103 for a reproducible activity!

Literacy: Have the group sit in a circle, and then pass a small beach ball to a youngster. To begin, play a recording of beach music and prompt little ones to pass the ball around the circle. Stop the music and have the child with the ball name a favorite beach activity or say any desired information about the beach. Continue in this manner until each child has had a turn.

I like to play in the sand!

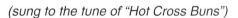 **Song:** Tell youngsters to pretend they are at the beach. Designate one area in your room to be the hot, sandy beach and a different area to be cool surf. Have little ones stand on the sandy beach and then lead them in performing the song shown.

(sung to the tune of "Hot Cross Buns")

Hot, hot sand; hot, hot sand.
It is so hot on your toes.
Hot, hot sand.

Hop up and down.

Cool, cool surf; cool, cool surf.
Now your toes are nice and cool.
Cool, cool surf.

Run on tiptoes to the surf.

Say "Ahhhh."

Literacy: Youngsters develop beach-themed vocabulary with this activity. Give each child a copy of page 102. Name something on the page and have each child point to the corresponding picture. Encourage students to share what they know about the item. Continue with the remaining items on the page. Then have each child color his page.

Note to the teacher: Use with the third activity on page 101.

Jolly Jellyfish

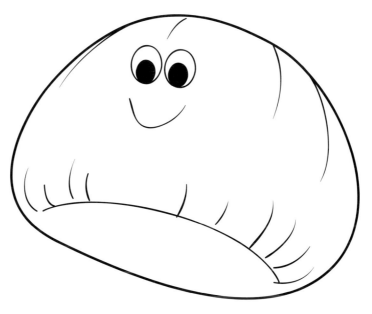

Note to the teacher: Have each child color a copy of the page. Then have her tear colorful strips of construction paper and glue them to the page to make tentacles on the jellyfish.

Ocean

Math: Cut out several copies of the fish patterns on page 106 so there is one cutout for each child plus two extras. Place one of each type of fish on opposite ends of a length of blue bulletin board paper. Distribute the remaining fish as you explain how fish that are alike live together in groups called schools. Invite each child, in turn, to place her fish in the correct school as you lead the remaining youngsters in reciting the rhyme shown.

> Little fish, little fish
> Off to school
> In the ocean,
> Nice and cool.

Literacy: Make a class supply of fish cutouts (pattern on page 106) and label each fish with a letter. Place the fish on a bedsheet (net). Youngsters hold the edges of the net and lift it in the air to toss the fish. Each child finds a fish and names the letter. Then students return the fish to the net and play another round.

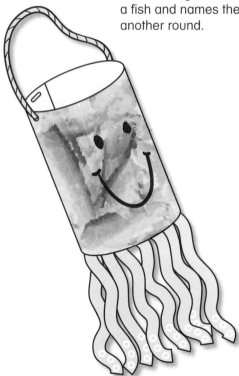

Art: To make this octopus windsock, invite each child to sponge-paint a sheet of white paper (body). When the paint is dry, encourage him to draw a face. Have him attach hole reinforcers (suckers) to eight lengths of crepe paper (arms). Then direct him to glue the arms to the lower edge on the back of the body. Help him form the body into a cylinder and staple it in place. Finally, have him punch two holes near the top of the octopus and help him attach a length of yarn for hanging.

Math: Attach hook side pieces of Velcro fasteners to the backs of five jellyfish cards (pattern on page 107). Place one jellyfish on a flannelboard and recite the first couplet of the rhyme shown. Have a child place another jellyfish on the flannelboard. Then recite the next couplet. Continue until all five jellyfish are on the flannelboard.

One little jellyfish in the ocean blue.
Along came another, and then there were two.
Two little jellyfish in the blue sea.
Along came another, and then there were three.
Three little jellyfish near the ocean floor.
Along came another, and then there were four.
Four little jellyfish ready to dive.
Along came another, and then there were five.
Five little jellyfish as happy as can be,
Moving around in the deep blue sea.

Science: This activity focuses on the senses of sight and sound. Help each child pour blue-tinted water and vegetable oil in a small water bottle. Then have him put metallic fish or sea creature confetti in the bottle. Secure the cap with tape. Encourage youngsters to move their bottles to make waves as they sing the song shown.

(sung to the tune of "The Wheels on the Bus")

The waves of the ocean go up and down,
Up and down, up and down.
The waves of the ocean go up and down
All day long.

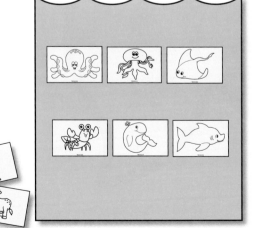

Science: Cut apart a copy of the jellyfish and animal cards on page 107 and place them in a small bag. Place a length of bulletin board paper (ocean) on the floor. (If desired, trim the paper as shown.) Prompt a child to take a card, show it to the group, and name the animal. If the animal lives in the ocean, direct the group to pretend to swim as the child puts the card on the ocean. If the animal does not live in the ocean, direct the group to be still and have the child set the card aside. Continue with the remaining cards.

Fish Patterns

Use with the third activity on page 61 and the
first and second activities on page 104.

TEC61310

TEC61310

Thematic Fun for Little Learners • ©The Mailbox® Books • TEC61310

Jellyfish Card
Use with the first and third activities on page 105.

Animal Cards
Use with the third activity on page 105.

TEC61310

TEC61310

TEC61310

TEC61310

TEC61310

TEC61310

TEC61310

TEC61310

Camping

Math: To prepare for this partner center, float a supply of foam fish in a water table. Set two small nets and two plastic pails nearby. Each child uses a net to scoop fish from the water and place them in his pail. After all the fish have been "caught," the youngsters count the fish in each pail and compare the amounts using words such as *more, less,* and *equal.*

Song: Get little ones ready for a camping unit with this toe-tapping ditty.

(sung to the tune of "If You're Happy and You Know It")

Let's go camping in the woods with all our friends.
Let's go camping in the woods with all our friends.
It's a camping holiday—don't forget mosquito spray.
Let's go camping in the woods with all our friends!

Literacy: In the center of the circle-time area, arrange cardboard tubes and tissue paper to represent the logs and flames of a campfire. For circle time during your camping theme, gather youngsters around the fire. While students are gathered, sing songs and read camping-themed books, such as *A Camping Spree With Mr. Magee* by Chris Van Dusen, *Maisy Goes Camping* by Lucy Cousins, and *Fred and Ted Go Camping* by Peter Eastman.

See page 111 for a reproducible activity!

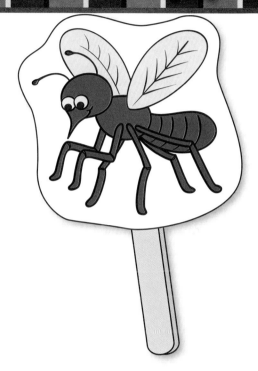

Science:
Students recognize body parts with this adorable idea. Have each child transform a copy of a mosquito pattern from page 110 into a stick puppet. Then have students move their mosquitoes through the air as they make a buzzing sound. Say, "Oh no! The mosquito landed on your arm!" Prompt each student to touch the mosquito to his arm. Then pretend to spray mosquito spray on youngsters' arms. Encourage students to once again move their mosquitoes through the air. Continue with other body parts.

Snack:
To make these no-melt s'mores, spread marshmallow fluff on a graham cracker. Then sprinkle miniature chocolate chips over the fluff. For a dipping option, have students mix the chips with the fluff and then dip graham sticks into the mixture!

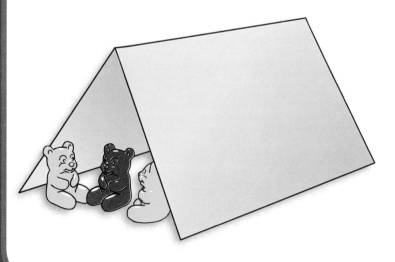

Making sets:
Give each child in a small group a few bear counters and a sheet of construction paper folded in half so it resembles a tent. Announce a number and direct each child to place a matching number of bears in her tent. Have youngsters check each member's work and make any necessary changes. Then have the group members roar like bears to signal that everyone has the correct answer. Continue using a different number each time.

Mosquito Patterns

Use with the first activity on page 109.

TEC61310

TEC61310

TEC61310

TEC61310

What's in the Tent?

_____

_____

_____

Note to the teacher: Have each child color a copy of the page. Then ask her what she thinks is in the tent. Write her words on her paper.   111

Colors

Math: Place at a center colorful copies of the present pattern on page 114 along with a basket containing bows of matching colors (one bow per present). A child sets out the presents. Then he removes a bow from the basket and places it on a matching present.

Snack: Give each child a serving of vanilla pudding and a spoon. Place drops of red, blue, and yellow food coloring on the pudding. Invite the youngster to gently swirl the pudding to mix the colors. Have her notice the new colors that are made when the colors are swirled together. Then encourage her to enjoy her tasty snack.

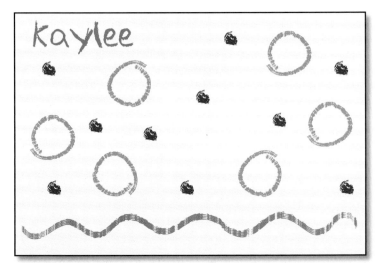

Fine motor: Provide each child with blank paper and a box of crayons. Give a direction such as "Use a blue crayon to write your name on your paper" or "Use a purple crayon to make dots on your paper." The child finds the correct crayon and completes the direction. Continue with each remaining crayon.

See page 115 for a reproducible activity!

Math: Place colorful cards of construction paper in a bag and gather youngsters into a circle. Take a card from the bag and ask youngsters to name the color. Then have youngsters look at their clothing and stand if they are wearing the color. Play a musical recording and invite each standing child to march around the circle to the beat of the music. Repeat the process with the remaining cards.

Song: After leading youngsters in singing this little ditty, name a color and invite each child to find an object of that color in the room.

(sung to the tune of "Row, Row, Row Your Boat")

Red, orange, yellow, blue,
Purple, pink, and gray.
Black and green and white and brown.
Find them all today.

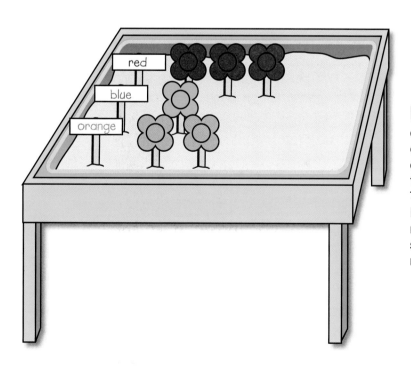

Literacy: To prepare, cut out colorful sets of the flower patterns on page 87. Attach each flower to a craft stick. For each color used, write the matching color word on a card. Then mount each card on a craft stick. Place the color words and flowers near a sand table. A child places each sign in the sand. Then she places the matching flowers beside each sign.

Present Pattern

Use with the first idea on page 112.

TEC61310

Cuddly Critters!

Thematic Fun for Little Learners • ©The Mailbox® Books • TEC61310

Note to the teacher: Have a child choose a crayon and name its color. Then have her use it to color one of the critters on a copy of the page. Continue in the same way with different colors until all the critters are colored.

Dinosaurs

Math: Puzzle-cut several different-color copies of the dinosaur pattern on page 118. Bury the resulting pieces in a sand table. Gather a small group of little archaeologists around the table and encourage them to dig to find the dinosaur pieces as they recite the chant shown. After all the pieces have been found, help youngsters put the pieces together to form whole dinosaurs. Then prompt the students to identify the color of each dinosaur.

> All day long we dig, dig, dig.
> We find dinosaurs that are big, big, big!

Literacy: Tell students that they are going to pretend to be dinosaurs. Say a dinosaur name (see list) and direct the group to repeat it. Then lead little ones in saying the name again as they stomp out the syllables. Encourage them to let out big dinosaur roars. Then repeat the activity using other dinosaur names.

Dinosaur Names

Allosaurus	Stegosaurus
Brachiosaurus	Triceratops
Iguanodon	Tyrannosaurus
Plateosaurus	Velociraptor

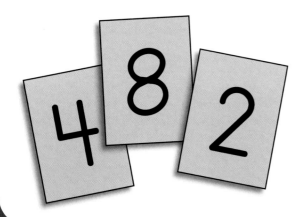

Math: Gather little ones in a large open area and invite them to pretend they are big dinosaurs. Hold up a number card. Then lead youngsters in counting to that number as they stomp like dinosaurs. Repeat the activity using a different number each time.

See page 119 for a reproducible activity!

Math: To prepare for this center activity, label each of four tagboard dinosaur cutouts (pattern on page 118) with a different shape. Place the dinosaurs and a supply of corresponding shape cutouts at a center. A child chooses a dinosaur and identifies the shape. Then he places matching shapes along the dinosaur's back so they resemble bony plates. He continues with the remaining dinosaurs.

Song: Celebrate dinosaurs big and small with this jaunty little tune!

(sung to the tune of "This Old Man")

Dinosaurs, dinosaurs!
See them stomp and see them roar.
Some are very big and some are very small.
Dinosaurs—I love them all.

Snack: Here's a healthy and simple dinosaur snack option! Give each youngster a small plate with dinosaur claws (thin apple slices), dinosaur bones (small pretzel sticks), and dinosaur teeth (triangular crackers). Then read youngsters a dinosaur-themed story such as *How Do Dinosaurs Say Good Night?* by Jane Yolen as students nibble on their treats.

Dinosaur Pattern
Use with the first activity on page 116 and the first activity on page 117.

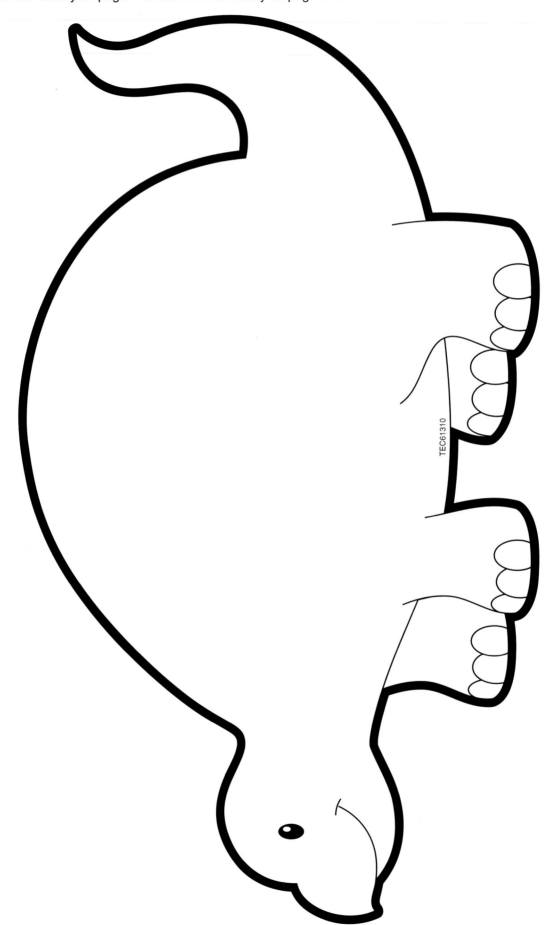

TEC61310

Hide-and-Seek

✂ Cut.

🖌 Glue to match.

Thematic Fun for Little Learners • ©The Mailbox® Books • TEC61310

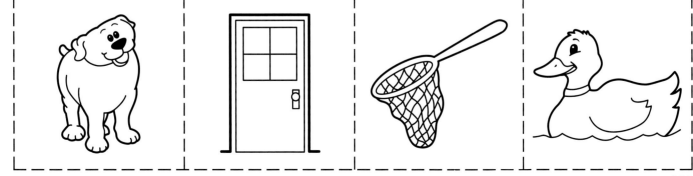

Math: Cut out several copies of the farm animal cards on page 122 and make large basic shape cutouts (animal pens). Choose a child and name an animal for him to find and the shape of the pen in which the animal should be placed. For example, you might say, "Find the pig and place it in the square pen." Continue until all the animals have been placed in pens.

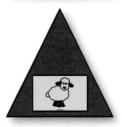

Song: Cut apart a copy of the farm animal cards on page 122 and stack them facedown. After singing the first verse of the song with little ones, take a card from the stack and display it. Then lead the group in singing the next verse of the song, inserting the animal's name and the sound it makes. Repeat the song with the remaining cards.

(sung to the tune of "The Wheels on the Bus")

Oh, who's in the barn out on the farm,
On the farm, on the farm?
Oh, who's in the barn out on the farm?
Who's in the barn?

The [cow]'s in the barn out on the farm,
On the farm, on the farm.
The [cow]'s in the barn out on the farm.
[Moo, moo, moo, moo].

Gross motor: Cut apart a copy of the farm animal cards on page 122 and place them in a small bag. Gather students in an open area of the room. Take a card from the bag and invite a youngster to name the animal. Guide little ones to determine how that animal moves and the sounds it makes. Then invite each child to mimic the animal's movements and sounds.

Literacy: Cut out a copy of the cards on page 123. Tell students that you went to a farm recently and saw some very strange things. Attach one of the cards to a sheet of chart paper and have students describe what they see. Repeat their descriptions, emphasizing the rhyming words. For example, you might say, "That's right! I saw a *goat* in a *coat!*" Prompt students to dictate a sentence about the picture as you write their words on chart paper. Continue with each remaining card.

That goat looks silly wearing a coat.

The pig with the wig went to the store.

Snack: Partially fill a clean plastic pail with prepared butterscotch pudding. Tell little ones that farmers mix several types of food together to make slop for pigs to eat. To make a much yummier batch of slop, invite each child to put a spoonful of granola, puffed rice cereal, and mini chocolate chips in the pail. Then encourage them to take turns using a large spoon to mix the slop. Serve each youngster a heaping helping of this tasty treat!

Living	Nonliving
sheep	barn
pig	tractor
corn	hoe
mouse	rocks
horse	dirt
	house
	horseshoe

Science: Label a chart with the headings shown. Tell students that living things grow and need air, food, and water. Nonliving things do not need these items. Have students name something they would find on a farm. Then encourage them to tell you whether this item is living or nonliving. Write the word beneath the correct heading. Continue with other suggestions.

Farm Animal Cards
Use with the first, second, and third activities on page 120.

TEC61310

TEC61310

TEC61310

TEC61310

TEC61310

TEC61310

TEC61310

TEC61310

TEC61310

TEC61310

TEC61310

TEC61310

Moon and Stars

Math: Write a number from 1 to 10 on each of ten star cutouts (pattern on page 126). Attach a jumbo moon cutout to the floor. Then make a path to the moon by attaching the stars to the floor in numerical order. Beginning with star 1, a little astronaut jumps on each star in order and says the number. He continues until he arrives at the moon. If desired, prompt the youngster to jump back down the number line and count backward!

Science: Pose the question "Where do the moon and stars go during the day?" Invite youngsters to share their thoughts. Then guide little ones to understand that the moon and stars are still in the sky but the moon is difficult to see during the day and the stars cannot be seen at all. To reinforce the idea, encourage little ones to use a white crayon to draw a moon and stars on a white sheet of paper. Then direct them to brush black watercolors over the paper to reveal the moon and stars.

I wish for a pizza.

Literacy: Lead youngsters in reciting the nursery rhyme shown. Then give each child a copy of the star pattern on page 126. In the center of the star, invite her to draw a picture to show a wish she would like to make. Have her dictate a sentence to match her illustration. Encourage her to share her wish with her classmates. If desired, display the stars on a board titled "Starry Wishes."

> Star light, star bright,
> The first star I see tonight—
> I wish I may, I wish I might
> Have the wish I wish tonight.

Arts and crafts: Provide plastic containers with different diameters and a shallow pan of gray paint. A child presses the rim of a container in the paint and then makes prints on white paper. He continues with a variety of containers. When the paint is dry, he cuts a moon shape from the paper and attaches it to a sheet of black paper. If desired, have him attach star stickers around the moon.

Song: Turn off the lights and invite little ones to pretend they are looking at the night sky as they sing this lively tune. If desired, post a few glow-in-the-dark stars around the room for effect.

(sung to the tune of "I've Been Working on the Railroad")

I've been looking at the night sky
Up above my head.
I've been looking at the night sky
Just before I go to bed.
I see lots of stars a-twinkling
And the big, white moon.
I could stare up there forever,
But it's bedtime soon.

Literacy: Cut out a copy of the cards on page 127 and place them in a bag. Make a supersize moon cutout and attach it to your wall. Have a child choose a card and name the picture. If the picture begins with /m/ like *moon,* have the child attach the card to the moon. Then lead students in reciting the rhyme. If the card does not begin with /m/, have the child set the card aside.

There's a [monkey] on the moon,
And I'm sure that you'll agree
That a [monkey] on the moon
Is as silly as can be!

Star Pattern

Use with the first and third activities on page 124.

TEC61310

TEC61310

TEC61310

TEC61310

TEC61310

TEC61310

TEC61310

TEC61310

TEC61310

TEC61310

TEC61310

TEC61310

TEC61310

Pets

Math: Cut apart a copy of the animal cards on page 130 and place them in a bag. Place a clean pet dish on the floor. Invite a youngster to choose a card and name the animal on it. If the animal would make good pet, have him place the card in the dish. If not, have him set the card aside. Continue with the remaining cards.

Social studies: Lead youngsters in a discussion about pet safety, guiding them to understand that not all pets are friendly and that they should always ask an owner before touching a pet. Then pair students and designate one partner as the pet owner. Give the pet owner a stuffed toy pet. Direct the other child to walk up to the owner and ask if she can pet his animal. Have youngsters switch roles and repeat the activity.

Literacy: Students practice speaking skills as they investigate the care of living things! Place a variety of items needed to care for different pets in a large shopping bag. Tell youngsters that you have just bought items for your new pets and you need their help determining how to use each one. Invite a student to take an item from the bag and show it to the group. Then ask volunteers to tell you what type of pet needs the item and how the item should be used. Continue with the remaining items.

Snack: Give a copy of page 131 to each child along with a cup including a mixture of circular and square-shaped cereal. A child sorts the cereal by shape onto the pet dishes. When the cereal is sorted appropriately, he nibbles on his snack!

Song: After singing this entertaining ditty with little ones, invite each child to name which pet is her favorite.

(sung to the tune of "Twinkle, Twinkle, Little Star")

Fur and scales and feathers too,
Which pet is the best for you?
One that meows or barks or tweets,
Dogs or cats or parakeets?
Fur and scales and feathers too,
Which pet is best for you?

Art: To make this adorable project, have each child draw a dog, cut it out, and attach it to a tub cutout as shown. Have her attach the cutouts to a sheet of construction paper and then make blue fingerprint bubbles around the rim of the tub and in the air. Fido's getting a bath!

Animal Cards

Use with the first activity on page 128.

TEC61310

TEC61310

TEC61310

TEC61310

TEC61310

TEC61310

TEC61310

TEC61310

Name _____

Dinnertime!

Thematic Fun for Little Learners • ©The Mailbox® Books • TEC61310

Note to the teacher: Use with the first activity on page 129.

Shapes

Snack: To make this circle snack, have each child put a scoop of circular cereal pieces, Ritz Bitz crackers, and M&M's Minis candies in a bag. Seal the bag and have the child shake the mix. Then, as she nibbles on her snack, prompt her to name the shape of each ingredient.

Song: Display a shape cutout and ask a volunteer to name it. Then lead little ones in performing this action song, using their fingers to make the shape in the air as they sing. Repeat the song using a different shape each time.

(sung to the tune of "If You're Happy and You Know It")

Make a [shape] in the air, in the air.
Make a [shape] in the air, in the air.
Make it large or make it small.
Make it anywhere at all.
Make a [shape] in the air, in the air.

Fine motor: Attach strips of masking tape to the floor to make a supersize square. Place a collection of toy cars near the square. Then encourage youngsters to visit the center and "drive" the cars along the shape. Periodically ask youngsters at the center the name of the shape. Each week, replace the tape to make a different shape.

See page 135 for a reproducible activity!

Literacy: Get little ones talking with this fun group activity! Make a copy of the spinner pattern on page 134. Help a volunteer spin the spinner using a pencil and paper clip as shown. Have the youngster name the shape. Then prompt her to find an object of that shape in the room. Repeat the activity several times.

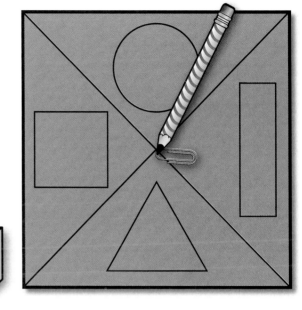

Math: Attach a class supply of shapes to the floor to form a circular path. Invite each child to stand behind a shape. Play a recording of music and prompt little ones to walk in a circle around the shapes. Stop the music and direct youngsters to name the shape they are standing behind. Start the music again to play another round.

Math: Place a variety of craft foam shapes in a large soup pot. Gather a small group of youngsters and tell them you made shape soup! Have each child ladle some of the soup into a bowl. Then prompt her to remove her shapes and sort them into piles. After she identifies each shape represented, have her place the soup back in the pot.

Spinner

Use with the first activity on page 133.

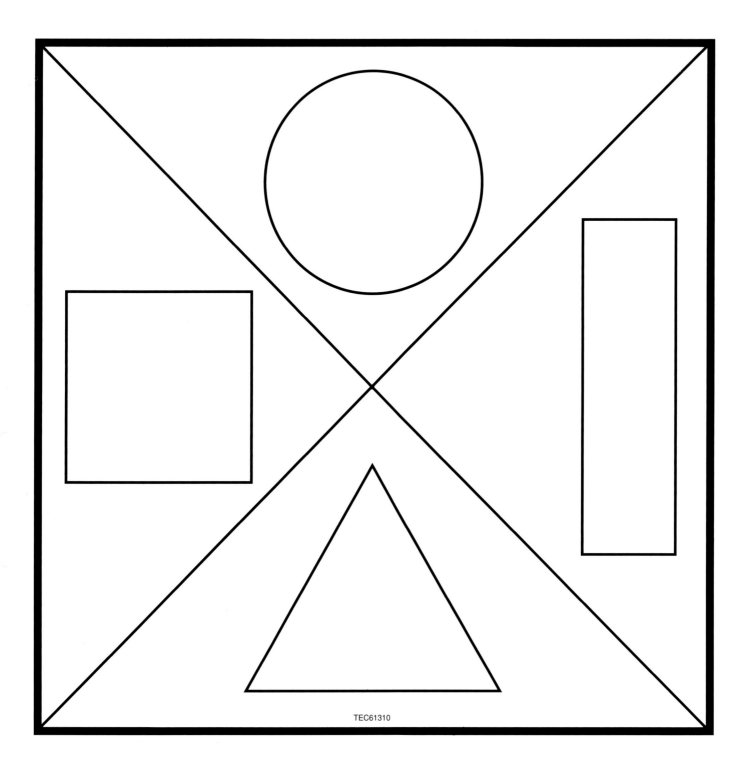

TEC61310

Party Time!

Cut.

Glue.

Teddy Bears

Art: To make this sweet art project, press a bear cookie cutter in a shallow pan of brown paint and then make a print on a piece of tan paper. Continue in the same way until a desired effect is achieved. Then drizzle yellow paint (honey) over the page. If desired, finish the masterpiece with several bee stickers!

Literacy: Have each child make a teddy bear stick puppet (patterns on page 138). Write a letter on the board and ask, "Teddy bear, teddy bear, what do you see?" Prompt youngsters to hold up their bears and say, "I see a [letter name] looking at me!" Erase the letter and repeat the activity using a different letter. If desired, use this activity to review numbers and shapes.

Snack: To prepare, slice bananas in half lengthwise. Have each child gently press bear-shaped crackers in a banana half so the bears appear to be in a boat! Encourage youngsters to nibble on their "bear-y" tasty snacks!

See page 139 for a reproducible activity!

Literacy: Cut out several copies of the large and small teddy bear cards on page 138. Label each large bear with an uppercase letter and each small bear with the corresponding lowercase letter. Place the bears at a center. A child chooses a large bear and pairs it with the small bear with the matching letter. He continues until all the cards are paired.

Literacy: Reinforce rhyming words with this chant! Have each child hold a teddy bear that he has brought from home. Then lead youngsters in saying the rhyme shown, inviting them to point to the parts of the teddy bear mentioned in the rhyme. At the end of the rhyme, encourage little ones to give their stuffed animals big bear hugs.

Teddy bear smile, so nice and sweet.
Teddy bear ears and teddy bear feet.
Teddy bear eyes so it can see.
Teddy bear, you belong to me!

Math: Youngsters identify colors and use size-related words with this activity. Cut out green, red, and blue copies of the large and small teddy bear cards on page 138. Arrange the cards in a grid as shown. Gather youngsters around the grid. Ask a child to find a large, red teddy bear. Prompt a child to point to the correct bear. Continue in the same way with different cards. For a different game option, have students close their eyes as you remove a teddy bear. Then have a student name the missing bear, identifying its size and color.

Large Teddy Bear Cards

Use with the second activity on page 136 and the first and third activities on page 137.

Small Teddy Bear Cards

Use with the first and third activities on page 137.

TEC61310

TEC61310

TEC61310

TEC61310

Teddy Count

 Count.

 Write the number.

ZOO

 **Literacy:** Youngsters use speaking and writing skills with this dramatic-play activity! Place a variety of plastic zoo animals and containers at your block center, along with paper and crayons. Youngsters work together to arrange the blocks to make enclosures for the animals. They use the containers for pretend food and swimming areas. Then they use the paper and crayons to make signs for the different animal enclosures.

 Song: Invite youngsters to name animals they might see at the zoo. Write students' responses on the board. Choose an animal from the list and then lead the group in singing the song shown. Sing the song several times, using a different animal from the list each time.

(sung to the tune of "If You're Happy and You Know It")

I'll be going to the zoo, and I can't wait!
I'll be going to the zoo, and I can't wait!
Do you think I'll see a [animal name]?
Oh, I hope I see a [animal name].
I'll be going to the zoo, and I can't wait!

Science: Youngsters match and identify animals with this activity. On a length of bulletin board paper, draw a simple zoo scene without animals. Then cut apart two copies of the cards on pages 142 and 143 and place them picture-side down near the scene. Invite a volunteer to turn over two cards and name the animals. If the animals match, have the child place the cards on the scene. If the animals do not match, have the child flip the cards over again.

See page 144 for a reproducible activity!

Literacy: Youngsters practice their speaking skills with this question-and-answer game. Display animal pictures or copies of the animal cards on pages 142 and 143. Pose a question such as "What animal in the zoo has a long neck?" or "What animal in the zoo roars?" Then ask a volunteer to use the pictures as a guide to help him answer the question.

> What animal in the zoo likes to climb trees?

> The monkey!

Math: Invite youngsters to sit in a circle. Help little ones begin a verbal *AB* pattern by having one child say "monkey," having his neighbor say "elephant," and then continuing the pattern around the circle. After each child has participated, repeat the pattern, replacing the words *monkey* and *elephant* with the sounds and motions those animals make.

Art: Encourage youngsters to name animals in the zoo that have stripes and animals that have spots. Then have each child celebrate these animals with some striped-and-spotted process art! Provide paper strips, torn pieces of animal print scrapbooking paper, circle cutouts, and hole punches. Then encourage students to glue items to a sheet of paper as desired. What a fun collage!

Zoo Animal Cards

Use with the third activity on page 140 and the first activity on page 141.

TEC61310

TEC61310

TEC61310

TEC61310

TEC61310

TEC61310

Zoo Animal Cards

Use with the third activity on page 140 and the first activity on page 141.

TEC61310

TEC61310

TEC61310

TEC61310

TEC61310

TEC61310

Just a Nibble

Note to the teacher: Give each child a copy of this page and a strip of brown paper. Have her color the picture as desired. Then direct her to tear pieces from the paper strip and glue them to the giraffe to make spots.

144